THE
CHANGING
FACE OF TODAY'S CUSTOMER

Strategies for Attracting and Retaining a
Diverse Customer and Employee Base
In Your Local Market

DOUG LIPP

Hickethier Publishing International
Fair Oaks, California

Published by
Hickethier Publishing International
3927 Edgevale Ct.
Fair Oaks, California 95628
www.douglipp.com

2nd Printing, 2007
ISBN: 0-9707648-2-0

Printed in the United States of America

Front cover illustration by Alison Zawacki
Jacket and book design by Burtch Hunter Design LLC

WHAT THEY'RE SAYING ABOUT DOUG LIPP AND THE CHANGING FACE OF TODAY'S CUSTOMER

"By embracing people of all backgrounds and nationalities, you can expand your business and create a whole new set of raving fan customers. This book shows you how to get beyond cultural barriers and tap into the power of diversity. A must-read for managers wanting to succeed in the new global economy."

• **Ken Blanchard**, co-author of *The One Minute Manager®* and *Full Steam Ahead!*

"Finally, a book on global service trends that is well-written, informative, and useful. In his book *The Changing Face of Today's Customer*, Doug Lipp shows businesses in North America how to create a unique experience for their local, multicultural customers and employees. *The Changing Face* is a much-needed addition to the customer service and leadership bookshelf."

• **Bob Gault**, President & Chief Operating Officer, Universal Orlando Resort

"The global marketplace is not only getting smaller, but considerably more competitive. Growing a business is more challenging than ever. *The Changing Face* shows us how to better understand our increasingly diverse customer's and employee's needs. By turning this cultural complexity into a competitive advantage, we can build loyalty and stay one step ahead of the market."

• **Pete Garcia**, Vice President, Latin America, Continental Airlines

"The issues, exercises, and case studies covered in *The Changing Face of Today's Customer* are very relevant in today's culturally-diverse business environment. In our efforts to listen to the voice of the customer, we must adapt our business processes in multicultural markets to better serve these clients. Your book opened my eyes to the need to conduct focus groups, customer interviews, and the in-depth research needed to serve diverse customers on their own terms."

• **Riccardo Ferracini**, Zone Manager, Acura Automobile Division

"At Northstar-at-Tahoe, our livelihood is dependent on two factors-the beautiful mountain environment, and the guests from all over the world who are drawn here. We treat both with the utmost respect. Doug Lipp's book *The Changing Face* captures the essence of respectful service, and helps guarantee that our business and others like it will be sustainable for many decades to come."

• **Debbie Kelly Hogan**, Director of Human Resources, Booth Creek
     Resorts/Northstar-at-Tahoe

"The devil is in the detail. In an ever increasingly diverse world, understanding and reacting to cultural nuances can make all the difference in developing loyal customers and employees. It takes special effort, but the companies that do it well win at the expense of those who don't. All successful businesses consistently add to their base of loyal customers and employees so they can grow faster than the overall marketplace. *The Changing Face* shows us how to do this in a world that is increasingly getting smaller and made up of people with and increasing variety of cultural backgrounds. The concepts and strategies that Doug Lipp presents to us are vital for winning in an increasingly complex and competitive world."

• **Jeff Simoneau**, Division President, FMC FoodTech

"Leading an enterprise in the 21st century means leading in a global environment. Even if your business never leaves the U.S., your customers and employees will increasingly come from different cultures, from around the globe. *The Changing Face* is the first hands-on, real world guide to understanding and serving people from diverse cultures, by an executive who has been there and done that. If you ever hope to serve Asian customers or lead Latin colleagues, you need to read this book. Now."

• **Gary Hoover**, founder, Hoovers Inc., author of Hoover's Vision

"Professionals in today's service industries continually strive for the excellence that sets them apart from competitors in a world where consumers have ever-more choices. In *The Changing Face of Today's Customer*, Doug Lipp provides case studies and in-practice techniques that serve as a blueprint for the caliber of exceptional service that keeps customers coming back."

• **Janine Chicourrat**, General Manager, The Lodge at Pebble Beach

"A 'Business of Caring' means getting involved—and promoting ways to help people help themselves. This is a key component of effective customer service, and an important concept in Doug Lipp's book *The Changing Face of Today's Customer*. This book is a must-read for any organization that serves the public and wants to serve it better."

• **Bryan Gerald**, Service Quality Leader, CIGNA HealthCare

DEDICATION

To my wife, Pam, and kids, Allison, Amanda and Keith. You're the best.

To my parents, Gordon and Pauline, for encouraging me to never give up.

To Lorrie, Davey and Carrie. Your continued support means everything.

To Nolan and Jennie Ahn, for giving me one of my first working experiences in a multicultural environment at Camp Naue (ees fo' keeds!), the YMCA of Kauai, Hawaii.

To Clifford H. Clarke. One of the pioneers of the study of intercultural communication, who also had the business acumen to found the Intercultural Relations Institute. It has been an honor working with you over these many years.

To Dr. Sheila Ramsey. One of the most gifted communicators in the field of intercultural relations. Your guidance over the years, both personal and professional, has been invaluable.

To Frank Lee. A true visionary in the field of leadership and management excellence.

To Jun, Yoshie and Michiru Akishige. My Japanese family.

CONTENTS

The Great Marketing Blunder

Driving Away Customers is This Easy!

Learning What Not to Do to Become More Culturally
   Sensitive

The Need to Think Globally

Exercises: Assessing Your "Global Service."
   How Do You Rate?

Understanding Culture: Getting Beneath the Cultural Iceberg

Principles of Intercultural Effectiveness

Exercise: The Effect of Culture and Common Sense

Using "Style Switching" to Adapt to Cultural Differences

Recognizing Corporate Culture

How Even the Little Things Can Create Cultural Conflicts

Breaking the Cultural Barrier

Exercises: What's Your Customer Service Cultural IQ?

#1) Failing to Apply the "When in Rome" Factor

#2) The Time Factor: Or, Are We Looking at the Same
   Calendar

#3) Language, The Great Equalizer Fallacy

FOREWORD

Global Mission, Not Yet Accomplished

The Changing Face of Today's Customer examines American entrepreneurship in the 21st century and finds it enthusiastic, yet still lacking in critical diversity skills.

While 20 years have passed since the Los Angeles Olympic Games I helped to orchestrate, the underlying issues of globalization, diversity, and unifying community have only intensified. We used the phrase "global village" often then, yet astoundingly enough, today the leadership of that village largely remains in the hands of old world thinkers, mostly male, mostly Caucasian. As *The Changing Face* author Doug Lipp points out, this practice needs to change.

For today's companies, honing the skills required to attract and maintain a diverse customer base simply isn't enough. In order to truly succeed, a business should mirror that customer base as well.

It only makes sense that as diversity grows within company ranks, a greater sense of empathy and tailored service will develop for its customer base, now more and more likely to comprise people born outside of the United States. From boardrooms to telephone service representatives, companies should better reflect the communities where they operate, and focus on globalization right in their own backyards. The mindset of think global, act local is essential for success.

Today much of my personal focus on service and community interaction centers around the Pebble Beach Company, highlighted as a case study of how to provide a truly global service experience in *The Changing Face*. Through Pebble Beach's internationally famous annual golf celebration, we attract a worldwide customer base. A high percentage of our global guests are repeat customers, and we work hard to provide them with a level of personalized service that will keep them coming back for many years to come.

Doug Lipp's book helps businesses of any size view the marketplace from a cultural perspective, instead of sheer customer number or dollars and cents. In my experience, this perspective is the only one that makes sense in these times, and I look forward to watching *The Changing Face* make its mark on the world of global business.

PETER UEBERROTH
June, 2003

INTRODUCTION

"Think globally to sell locally" could easily be the title of this book. It is about providing good customer service to individuals from different cultures. It is also about building and maintaining a culturally diverse group of employees that can serve these customers. It does not mean you have to take your business overseas to expose yourself to multiple cultures, overseas has come to you. There continues to be a tremendous influx in the number of immigrants to the North American continent and the people who make up these many cultures are your potential customers and employees. Many have already browsed through your stores, worked for you, visited your websites, contacted your customer service call centers and purchased your products. The question is: are you doing what it takes to both attract and keep them? Some companies are, some companies aren't. This book shares examples of cross-cultural success and failure, and introduces a number of strategies to ensure long-term success in this new era of a shrinking business globe. There is one prerequisite, however. You must be open to re-thinking your notions of what makes a business, product or leader successful.

We are exposed to the following words on a daily basis: *customer service*, *leadership*, *management* and *international business*. They are quite familiar, so most of us have opinions about what they mean. In fact, in the 30-plus years that I have been in business, I have yet to come across a person who doesn't have his or her own strong definition of the meaning of these words and how they can be applied on the job. Of course, having a good understanding of these words or concepts is not a guarantee of effective application in the workplace. As a result, we have a tremendous number of books, university courses, business seminars and other educational materials devoted to these topics. There has been a generous overlapping of the research of academicians with the real-time experiences of thousands of professional managers and industry leaders. As a result, those who have the desire to learn more about these concepts can explore any number of sources, ranging from scholarly tomes brimming with the results of empirical research about how to build and maintain one's business, to anecdotal articles extolling the virtues of certain management styles, written by any number of well known business leaders with years' of experience. In essence, there is an abundance of time-tested models of business excellence for us to examine, learn from and apply, if we so desire.

Now, consider a second set of words: *intercultural communication, culture, cross-cultural communication* and *multicultural effectiveness*. In the past decade, these have popped up with increasing frequency in the mass media, business schools, various forms of entertainment, and even elementary schools. Yet, more often than not, people react to these words with a look of puzzlement. Many have a vague idea of the meaning of the words themselves, perhaps they even attended a course or read a book about "something dealing with cross-cultural communication", yet are caught flat footed about how to apply them in the workplace. Unfortunately, relative to the first set of words, there has not been the rich sharing of research, and it's application, between the worlds of academia and business with this second set of words and concepts. The result? A general lack of understanding about what intercultural effectiveness is and how it plays out in the workplace. To be sure, there are vast numbers of wonderful books and articles, written by scholars and lifelong students of intercultural communication, that are full of useful information...as long as you can understand what is being said. Rich with research results, data and scholarly analysis, much of the information in these books and articles is hard to decipher, harder yet to apply on the job.

My goal is to blend the worlds of academic research and business practicality into a book that is accurate in it's message, compelling to read and useful as a tool to help you implement new, culturally appropriate, strategies. Those who accept the global nature of domestic business, then take steps to adjust, will realize tremendous opportunities to expand their businesses beyond traditional customer and employee groups. It means, however, being willing to take a fresh look at one's product, service or leadership approach from a new perspective, a *cultural* perspective. I hope this book helps in that regard.

DOUG LIPP
November, 2006, Sacramento, California

THE CHANGING FACE OF TODAY'S CUSTOMER

CHAPTER ONE

THE WORLD IS SHRINKING. IS YOUR BUSINESS EXPANDING?

There is an interesting irony occurring in business today. More and more companies are chasing the same customers and, as a result, maintaining or gaining market share seems to be a futile exercise. Let's call the market the "customer pie." And, whether by design or benign neglect, organizations and companies that serve the customers making up this pie are scratching their collective heads to come up with new and improved ways to continually slice, into smaller pieces, a pie that appears to them to be the same size.

The irony is this. The pie is not the same size. It is, in fact, getting larger. Yes, the number of groups who rely on the customer pie for their subsistence is expanding dramatically. But so is the pie.

The problem? How companies choose to look at the pie and those customer groups that make the pie what it is.

Due to advances in communication, the spread of the

Internet, e-commerce and the ease of travel, our globe is essentially shrinking. As a result, more than ever before, we are coming into contact with people from different cultural backgrounds, even if we don't leave our "home" countries. So, as a provider of a service or product, a tremendous opportunity exists to target groups of people you haven't considered in the past.

The pie is, indeed, getting bigger.

But the big problem in numerous companies is many people just don't understand how to properly deal with the expectations of someone from a different culture and end up squandering tremendous business opportunities. Mistakes are not limited to those on the front lines, the customer service employees. Everyone in the company needs to pitch in to make this work, including the engineers, sales people, administrative support staff and the organization's executive leadership. Also, it doesn't matter whether existing or potential customers are living overseas, visiting from abroad, or living close by. The point is that in addition to language differences, they have different interests, needs, desires, priorities, ways of doing business, and other cultural expectations that should be taken into account.

In short, providing good customer service to individuals from different cultures is not only good business, but a powerful way for any company to gain leverage against competitors and increase their share of the pie. Opportunities abound for those companies that grow beyond the culturally myopic, "we know what is best for you" or "one size fits all" mentalities that come from cultural ignorance or arrogance. Learning how to appeal to diverse customers, whether foreign-born or from different cultural communities in the domestic market, will give any company a tremendous competitive advantage in today's increasingly global economy.

THE GREAT MARKETING BLUNDER

Having this knowledge is a way to avoid major blunders, such as what happened at the beginning of a recent ski season at a major California ski resort. The customer service and marketing departments could have easily avoided the problem with the proper cross-cultural training and advance preparation. The problem began after the market research team identified the large Chinese population in the San Francisco Bay area as an untapped market for skiing. To appeal to this market, the marketing department saturated the community during the summer off-season with ads promoting the resort and the fun of skiing, hoping to attract community members to the resort that winter. The marketing people thought they had done their homework, since they had the ads translated into perfect Chinese and ran them in the local Chinese newspapers and magazines. The ads offered the following deal: "Bring this advertisement to our rental department and receive a 2 for 1 discount on rental equipment for the day."

But the marketing department never ran the ads by the customer service people who would be dealing with their customers or their managers to make sure they were prepared to respond. As a result, when the Chinese customers poured into the rental department with their discount coupons, disaster struck, since the resort had not been prepared on how to properly respond to this new clientele. The rental shop wasn't staffed with anyone who spoke Chinese, although many of the older customers knew no English. In addition, the employees hadn't been trained on how to interpret the coupons, which were written in Chinese. Since none of them could read or speak Chinese, all they could understand was the non-Chinese portion of the coupon, which said: "50% off." But they didn't know what this meant. They didn't know what products were marked 50 percent off or if the coupon applied to all of them. They also didn't know whether the coupon was good for just one person, for a whole family, or for how long.

Within minutes of the store's opening, the employees were in a state of panic and arguing with the customers over the offer. Since the customers spoke little or no English, many simply didn't understand the problem. Finally, a few bilingual customers (many of whom were children) stepped forward to interpret and, with their help, the customer service people managed to work out some general agreement about what they were charging the customers.

But then, another complication arose, because the resort had not been forewarned by the marketing department to anticipate the increased demand for certain products by customers who were smaller than their average-sized customer. The shop soon ran out of smaller-sized boots, skis, poles and snowboards before most of the customers had been helped. Thus, the morning ended with many frustrated customers walking out the door without renting any skiis, thereby undermining the success of the marketing department's well-thought out and executed media campaign.

The key reasons for the foul-up? First, there was a lack

of communication between the marketing department and the customer service department about their plans to reach out to a different cultural market. Secondly, the customer service department hadn't been properly prepared by either the marketing department or top management to deal with a multicultural customer. They lacked both the proper training and the personnel with the right skills, which required a knowledge of Chinese and Chinese culture to offer the proper customer service.

Unfortunately, this type of customer service nightmare has become increasingly common in many industries. Cultural insensitivity dramatically reduces the size of the customer pie. When an organization isn't responsive or sensitive to the differences and special needs and interests of members of diverse cultural groups, they create a negative cycle that shows up in the following ways:

- First, they create a corporate culture or environment that doesn't welcome employees who may come from different cultural groups. The employee population doesn't diversify as much as it should, and the result is a lack of originality and creativity in the development of new products, services and marketing strategies.

- Second, given the narrow focus of the product line or service strategy, they discourage new customers from different cultural groups from purchasing a product or using a service in the first place. Or, after a purchase, the customers may be disappointed in the product or service they do receive and don't continue using or buying it.

- Third, as this cycle reaches completion, the company looks at the small number of customers from different cultural backgrounds they are serving and use the data to support this argument: Why should we develop culturally appropriate product lines and service strategies, then hire bi-lingual employees to service this population, if the target audience doesn't buy what we're selling?

It's obvious where this is headed.

DRIVING AWAY CUSTOMERS IS THIS EASY!

Cultural insensitivity can be equally destructive when it occurs on the phone, as well as in person, resulting in conflict and upset customers and employees. That's what happened when Mr. Songkhalarb Sanitwongwaaryudthaya, a recent émigré from Thailand, got an advertising flyer in the mail from Mobile Cellular, a fictitious name for a well-known North American cellular telephone company, touting it's wonderful cellular telephone service. He was delighted that the flyer was written in his native Thai language, so he felt the company was especially sensitive to his cultural group by taking the extra effort to create an advertisement in a language not usually used in the U.S. Although he had grown accustomed to life in North America and his English had steadily improved, he appreciated reading something in his native tongue.

Thus, he was already prepped to be receptive to the offer, and he called the number listed in the ad, eager to learn more about the offer of extensive free minutes and no roaming charges. But almost immediately, his enthusiasm was dampened when he encountered a telephone rep in the customer service department who couldn't understand him. The conversation went something like this:

Customer Service Rep: "Thank you for calling Mobile Cellular. How can I help you?"

Songkhalarb Sanitwongwaaryudthaya (Customer): "Uh... hello?

Customer Service Rep: "Hello, this is Mobile Cellular. How can I help you?"

Customer: "Uh... can.... you teach me.... about..."

Customer Service Rep: "Please speak up, I can't hear you very well."

(Rep interrupted customer, spoke loudly, didn't soften the statement with "could you please...")

Customer: "Please teach me about.... your new...mobile program ..."

Customer Service Rep: "I'll connect you with new accounts."

(Rep cut off customer and immediately transferred him to another department without asking, "Would that be all right?" Also, didn't set up the transfer for success. The rep could have prepared the new accounts rep for the transfer by giving the name of the customer and giving a "heads up" about the customer's language difficulties.)

New Accounts Customer Service Rep: "New accounts. How can I help you?"

Customer: "Please teach me about.... your new......mobile program..."

New Accounts Customer Service Rep: "Our new what? Could you say that again?"

(Rep could have said, "I'm sorry, I couldn't hear very well, could you say that again?")

Customer: "Do you speak Thai?"

New Accounts Customer Service Rep: "No, I can barely speak English (laughs at own joke). Now, what'zit you need?"

(This last comment is rude, insensitive and just adds to the frustration the customer already feels due to the previous comments.

The conversation continued like this for another frustrating five minutes. By the end, Mr. Sanitwongwaaryudthaya was very upset the company didn't have a representative who could speak Thai, since he had expected this after getting a flyer in the Thai language. He was also upset that the customer service rep had treated him with a lack of respect, even cracking a joke about his lack of knowledge. At the same time, the customer service representative was irritated because this call was taking far too long, much more than the average three-minute call time at the call center, and she knew her supervisor would not be pleased.

Then, making matters worse, after the customer service rep was finally able to overcome the language and cultural barrier and was ready to close the sale, she encountered another hurdle because the paperwork itself wasn't set up to respond to the customer's needs. The conversation went like this:

New Accounts Customer Service Rep: "So, could I have your name to start your new account?"

Customer: "My name is Songkhalarb Sanitwongwaaryudthaya."

New Accounts Customer Service Rep: "Could you repeat that?"

Customer: " Songkhalarb Sanitwongwaaryudthaya."

New Accounts Customer Service Rep: "How is that spelled?"

Customer : " S-o-n-g-k-h-a-l-a-r-b S-a-n-i-t-w-o-n-g-w-a-a-r-y-u-d-t-h-a-y-a "

New Accounts Customer Service Rep: "I'm sorry, sir, our customer information form only allows 20 spaces for names. Do you mind if we abbreviate your name?"

Needless to say, this was the last straw for Mr. Sanitwongwaaryudthaya. He felt insulted and demeaned that he couldn't use his full name, which, in his culture, as in many, was a source of honor and pride. As a result, he decided to forget about purchasing the cellular phone service and hung up, leaving the customer service representative feeling equally upset and thinking she had just endured another demanding customer with unrealistic expectations.

This is just one example of many unsuccessful interactions between the customer service department and the targeted Asian consumer base the Mobile Cellular marketing department was trying to reach. As a result, it's not surprising that the number of new customers added due to the company's expensive marketing and advertising campaign was far less effective than expected. Despite a high number of calls from prospective customers for information, the percentage of sales closed was far lower than what was projected as being successful.

LEARNING WHAT NOT TO DO TO BECOME MORE CULTURALLY SENSITIVE

While these examples of problems with insensitive in-person and telephone customer service come from companies reaching out to Asian customers, this type of scenario occurs all too frequently in today's global business age. Companies strive to open up new markets for their products or services, only to be tripped up somewhere in the company by employees who don't understand the diverse customers in this market and thereby fail to respond to them properly. Even when top management is committed to being responsive to cultural differences and understands what the company should do to broaden its reach to that market (such as shown by the sensitivity of the marketing department in these stories), the approach won't work if the front-line employees aren't on board. They are the ones providing that immediate contact with the customer in the store, the office, or on the phone, and if they lack the sensitivity and cultural awareness and aren't trained in what to do, they will make many mistakes. And worse, they may not even be aware of what they are doing wrong, so they can't improve.

Thus, to illustrate the range of mistakes that these front line people can easily make, let's look more closely at what happened at Mobile Cellular.

The company started off doing everything right by carefully preparing for its aggressive marketing campaign. The marketing department spent six months analyzing potential new domestic markets and used this research to identify the rapidly growing immigrant population as having the highest potential. It also identified the major countries supplying most of this growth, including Taiwan, Hong Kong, India, Vietnam, Thailand, and Pakistan.

Then, to tap into this fast-growing market, the marketing department teamed up the advertising department at the company to jointly create an advertising campaign to appeal to this potentially huge group of new customers.

Again, these departments made all the right moves. They designed the advertising campaign in several Asian languages and they carefully selected the TV and radio stations, Internet news groups, e-mail addresses, magazines and newspapers targeted to this market. Additionally, the advertising department was careful to hire professional translators to transform their English messages into the appropriate Asian languages.

As projected, the response from the targeted communities was very strong, and the marketing and advertising departments were ecstatic over the success of their campaign in introducing their services to many new potential customers. But then, that's when the company's targeted marketing strategy campaign broke down, because the customer service department did not share the same preparation or cultural awareness, so they weren't able to respond properly, as illustrated by the telephone call between Mr. Sanitwongwaaryudthaya and the customer service representatives. The customer service reps simply were not ready for the onslaught of calls from the local Asian market and they made a large number of mistakes in many areas of customer service. Many of these were because the company itself had not provided the customer service department's supervisors and employees with the appropriate support and training so they would know what to do.

These mistakes ranged from not knowing the language and culture, to not having the appropriate scripts and forms to use in responding to customers when they called.

The following list illustrates the major errors by both the customer service department and the company as whole – while the opposite is what a culturally aware customer service department and company should do.

- The company had no plan for hiring and training bilingual representatives, and due to budget limitations, the company had no plan to hire more reps in the future.

- The leadership of the company failed to adjust long-standing policies to the realities of a new customer base. For example, the customer service department did not adjust its call center policy of handling all calls within three minutes, even though the customer service reps found their calls with Asian customers took an average of five minutes to overcome language difficulties or to provide additional explanations of the services offered. The problem with this policy is that it was developed based on an assumption that most customers would be able to speak English or Spanish, so the department had staffed up with plenty of English and Spanish-speaking representatives. But then, because the policy wasn't changed – and the company didn't give supervisors in the customer service department the authority or guidance to change the policy – the reps felt a great deal of pressure to handle the calls within three minutes. As a result, the customer service representatives tried to rush through the calls and felt tremendous pressure when the calls went beyond the three-minute limit. This time limit was a goal long revered within the company and was the basis for the performance reviews of the customer service representatives, since they were evaluated more on how quickly they processed their calls, and not as much on the quality of the call itself. The outcome was bad for everyone. While the customer service representatives grew impatient and frustrated during the time they spent on longer calls with the new immigrant customers, their supervisors were hounding them because the calls were "getting too long." The result? Abrupt or rude service providers angry with customers who couldn't speak their language, and frustrated customers who weren't getting answers to their questions. Thus, sometimes even the longer calls weren't long enough and ended up with fewer sales.

- The company didn't provide the customer service representatives and supervisors with any training about the targeted customers' cultural backgrounds in the Asian market. As a result, neither the supervisors nor reps were prepared for any culturally based requests, and often thought of them as simply unusual requests from individual customers, rather than ones common for members of a different cultural group. They had no idea, for example, that many callers from Taiwan and Hong Kong would ask the company to include the number eight somewhere in their new telephone number, because the Chinese believe the number brings good luck and prosperity. But then, when many did, the reps commonly brushed them off with the insensitive reply: "I'm sorry. You can only get what's available and we have no more telephone numbers with the digit 'eight' left." Yet, had the reps and the company been prepared, they could have reserved a pool of such numbers for these customers.

- The company also did not provide the staff any training in how to effectively communicate with non-native speakers of English, so the reps often had trouble understanding what the customers were saying. For example, they had no training in recognizing the different accents or common speech patterns, so they weren't prepared to recognize predictable accents or patterns of speech. For example, the tonal nature of Chinese can make it sound somewhat confrontational to a listener who doesn't know this pattern. So, while learning a new language as an adult is next to impossible, learning patterns such as tones or pace are easily learned.

- The company also failed to expand or alter the customer information sheets to accommodate the needs of customers with longer names. However, such a modification was necessary because the first and last names of many customers, particularly in the case of immigrants from Southeast Asia and Malaysia, were longer than the standard names in North America. As a result, the customer service representatives couldn't fill in these customers' complete names in the company's "request for new service" application forms. So the reps took the approach of asking new customers to abbreviate their names to fit into the number of spaces, which angered many of them. And then there were often longer calls as customers tried fruitlessly to protest this policy, and in many cases the customers were so upset, they declined to purchase their cellular phone service from the company.

- While the customer service department supervisors worked out a standard script for the reps to use, they never analyzed it to determine how a non-native speaker of English would receive it. They didn't notice that some of the words and phrases used were unfamiliar, unclear or even insulting, because they didn't consider the meanings from their customer's point of view.

- There was no "live" training during which the customer service representatives had the opportunity to interact with people who represented the targeted customer groups. Thus, armed with their scripts and no training, the customer service representatives eagerly answered their telephones, but promptly overwhelmed the new customers by speaking too rapidly and not stopping to allow for any "space" during which the customer would have time to: A) collect his/her thoughts, B) translate his question from his native tongue into English and, C) ask questions!

As these examples illustrate, not only the front-line employees, but also the supervisors and top management at Mobile Cellular, apart from the marketing and advertising departments, overlooked virtually every way to properly deal with members of the cultures targeted for their business expansion plans. Ironically, the company designed its new marketing strategy to appeal to these cultural groups, but then failed to take their linguistic and cultural needs into account in creating a response to them that would work. In short, the company, from management to customer service supervisors and representatives, failed to think at the global and multi-cultural level and their local sales suffered as a result.

THE NEED TO THINK GLOBALLY

This age of trans-border commerce, coupled with expanding numbers of foreign-born customers in our heretofore domestic markets, demands that companies and their customer service personnel think globally to sell locally, rather than losing existing customers and many potential customers, because they don't understand what people from different cultures want and expect. While many companies – from executives to front line employees—lack this understanding due to cultural ignorance, where they are unaware of the need to pay attention to difference, some companies don't even think it is necessary to adapt their goods or services to different types of customers. That's because they mistakenly think today's globalized world has created a standardized culture based on American values. They are ethnocentric, and have a limited, "We know what is best for you," and "one size fits all" approach. Such an attitude is worse than just being culturally unaware or ignorant. Rather, it represents a cultural arrogance that is a prescription for economic disaster in a culturally diverse global world.

While most companies and individuals simply act out of cultural ignorance, like the companies introduced in this section, the ultimate results are the same. Without the knowledge or consideration of cultural differences, your company won't meet the unique needs of customers from multicultural, international, and diverse backgrounds, so you will mistakenly drive them away or into the arms of the competition.

In short, providing good customer service to individuals from different cultures is not only good business, but is a powerful way to gain leverage against competitors. The companies that know how to appeal to diverse customers, whether foreign-born or from different cultural communities within the country, will gain a tremendous competitive advantage in today's increasingly global world.

The pie is growing. Is your slice getting larger?

EXERCISE: ASSESSING YOUR "GLOBAL SERVICE"

In general, how would you rate yourself, your team or your organization with regard to your global service approach? This exercise is divided into two parts, with four questions in each section.

Part I asks you to identify some of your personal strengths and areas for improvement regarding cultural sensitivity to customers and employees. Part II asks you to identify some of your organizational strengths and areas for improvement in these same areas. Both sections ask for qualitative, as well as quantitative, answers. For the quantitative questions, rate yourself, your department, and your company on a scale of 1 to 10, with 1 being very poor and 10 being outstanding service. Make copies of this scale so you can do these ratings separately. You can also do this exercise individually or as a group over time, say every month or two, so you can compare how you or your group are doing.

GLOBAL SERVICE—HOW DO YOU RATE?

Part IA: Strengths

1) List two approaches you personally use that demonstrate a culturally sensitive approach with your *customers*.

A)_____

_____

_____

B)_____
_____
_____

2) Rate yourself on the following scale, (1 is low, 10 is high) by answering the following: "I am sensitive to the needs of my culturally diverse *customers*."

1   2   3   4   5   6   7   8   9   1 0

3) List two approaches you personally use that demonstrate a culturally sensitive approach with your *employees or co-workers*.

A)_____
_____
_____

B)_____
_____
_____

4) Rate yourself on the following scale, (1 is low, 10 is high) by answering the following: "I am sensitive to the needs of my culturally diverse *employees/co-workers*."

1   2   3   4   5   6   7   8   9   10

GLOBAL SERVICE—HOW DO YOU RATE?

Part IB: Areas To Improve

5) List two ways you could improve your approach to your culturally diverse *customers*.

A)_____

_____

_____

B)_____

_____

_____

6) List two ways you could improve your approach to your culturally diverse *employees/co-workers*.

A)_____

_____

_____

B)_____

_____

_____

GLOBAL SERVICE—HOW DOES YOUR COMPANY RATE?

Part IIA: Strengths

7) List two approaches your company/department uses that demonstrate a culturally sensitive approach with *customers*.

A)_____

_____

_____

B)_____

_____

_____

8) Rate your company/department on the following scale, (1 is low, 10 is high) by answering the following: "My company/department is sensitive to the needs of our culturally diverse *customers*."

1   2   3   4   5   6   7   8   9   10

9) List two approaches your company/department uses that demonstrate a culturally sensitive approach with *employees*.

A)_____

_____

_____

B)_____

_____

_____

10) Rate your company/department on the following scale, (1 is low, 10 is high) by answering the following: "My company/department is sensitive to the needs of our culturally diverse *employees/co-workers*."

1   2   3   4   5   6   7   8   9   10

GLOBAL SERVICE—HOW DOES YOUR COMPANY RATE?

Part IIB: Areas To Improve

11) List two ways your company/department could improve its approach to your culturally diverse *customers*.

A)_____

_____

_____

B)_____

_____

_____

12) List two ways your company/department could improve its approach to your culturally diverse *employees/co-workers*.

A)_____

_____

_____

B)_____

_____

_____

So, how did you do? This exercise posed questions that were broad-based, with the goal of raising your awareness to general trends in your or your organization's approach to the topic of global customer service. Admittedly, these scores are not scientific and, since they are a self assessment, can be skewed. However, if you gave it an honest try and gathered the opinions of others in your company, you undoubtedly identified some interesting trends. Identifying these trends now will help you get more out of the rest of the book. Consider this a very general pre-test to warm you up. The next chapter will get into a lot more detail about culture and the exercises will ask you much more specific questions.

CHAPTER TWO

THIS THING CALLED CULTURE: CULPRIT OR ASSET?

What is culture, and why should we pay attention to it? Why doesn't the *"one size fits all"* approach work with people of different cultures? As a business, how can we expand our business and profits by catering to diverse cultures?

Although much has been written about culture and intercultural effectiveness, many business executives and managers don't understand how to effectively incorporate knowledge of culture into business success. This chapter discusses how to provide global customer service by understanding culture and how to use this knowledge to be successful with both domestic and international employees and customers from different cultural backgrounds.

THIS THING CALLED CULTURE

The in-depth understanding of culture is what the social science of anthropology is all about. It teaches us that people are affected by the standards and norms of the society in which they grow up, live and work. The result is the totality of the person's identity and relationship to others, which we call "culture." It includes all of the values, beliefs, ways of behaving, patterns of thinking, and styles of communication that include the members of a particular culture. Each culture can represent different ways of responding to the world, and those responses have developed due to past traditions and present day realities. By taking these differences into account, those in customer service can have a better ability in relating to people of different cultural backgrounds.

Each of us is, of course, a unique individual with our own way of thinking, behaving, valuing, and communicating. We also have our personal beliefs as to what is right and wrong, natural or unnatural, and acceptable or unacceptable. Nevertheless, despite our individual uniqueness, the culture in which we have grown up or have become familiar with is an extremely powerful influence. As a result, we can identify common values and patterns of thinking and behaving, which are shared by the members of any national, linguistic, religious, gender, generational, socioeconomic, ideological, or ethnic group.

This is true of cultures all over the world, not only the ones with a relatively homogeneous population, such as Japan or Germany, but of diverse, multi-ethnic societies like the U.S. Even though we have a broad mainstream culture featured in our films and popular magazines, there are a vast number of cultures and subcultures—and complicating the matter, people belong to different groups based on many characteristics, from race and ethnicity to religion, age, and social interests. At the same time, racial and ethnic factors are especially powerful, as are the influences due to coming from a foreign society where the ways of life, thought, and language are so different.

These cultural forces are extremely strong influences, and members of each group are expected to live by its rules and customs. You will notice that if you think about the many cultures you and your friends and associates participate in. You learn that you will gain social approval and the rewards of that culture if you behave in the manner accepted. Or if you don't, if you "step out of line" and ignore the rules of behavior, you will encounter disapproval and various forms of punishment, from just a rebuke or look of disfavor to exclusion from the group.

Though many people don't realize this, all of us have lived and worked in different cultures, even if we have never left our home states. Just going from elementary to middle school to high school represents a culture shift, in that the culture of one school can be quite different from another. Such differences even include everyday items as: What time did school start? Did you get a recess break every two hours or have to wait longer? What about the cafeteria and the type of food served?

The same cultural shift occurs in transferring from one department or business unit to another, even within the same company. Each company and all of the divisions within the company represent different cultures. You can see these differences in places, too. The culture of a small town is vastly different from a large city; the culture of the north or west is vastly different from the south. And so are the differences between one state and another. Thus, even if the inhabitants of these different locations all speak the same language, their respective cultures can be dramatically different.

UNDERSTANDING CULTURE AND GETTING BENEATH THE CULTURAL ICEBERG

By understanding people of different cultural backgrounds, your company and employees can provide far better customer service and gain greater customer satisfaction and sales.

Let's see how this can be done by looking at what happens when people with different cultural backgrounds interact with each other, whether in person, over the phone, via e-mail, or by fax. When they do, their communication represents a small percentage of who they are and what they are saying, since each person brings to the exchange a wide range of cultural differences in the language they use, the words they say, their meanings, and other qualities.

In effect, the communication represents the tip of an iceberg, and the more personal the communication, the more the iceberg is revealed. This split between what is on the surface and what lies beneath it is expressed in the Cultural Iceberg model, shown on pages 34 and 35, in which the iceberg is used as a metaphor for culture. This is an apt metaphor, since most of an iceberg—perhaps 80 to 90 percent of it—is underwater, so the portion above water is just a small fraction of the whole thing. Likewise, in the human cultural context, the portion of an interaction or communication that is above the water represents those things we can become aware of by using our five senses of sight, hearing, touch, taste and smell. So, by observing what goes on "above the waterline," we can identify any number of behavioral or environmental differences from one culture to another. A complete list is impossible to create, but the following captures some of the more applicable issues as related to the topic of this book:

- Language
- Word choice
- Skin color
- Clothing
- Ritualistic behaviors, from hugging, to handshakes to bowing
- Style of address and greeting people, from being more formal with first time acquaintances to more informal with old friends
- Work hours
- Laws: Hard and fast or negotiable?
- "Appropriate" tone of voice in different situations and with different people
- Directness of eye contact
- Eating habits
- Leadership style
- Aromas
- Sense of time (such as reflected in different speeds of walking and talking)
- Architecture
- Meeting management
- "Proper" treatment of customers
- Modes of transportation

Many of the observable things listed here differ by culture, but so can the underlying values, beliefs, meanings, and other unseen internal characteristics reflected by these outer differences. Thus, in order to get an even better picture of what makes a cultural counterpart "tick," we need to put on our SCUBA tanks, dive into the water and take a look at the rest of the iceberg ... the 80 to 90 percent we haven't yet seen!

As illustrated in the iceberg diagram, the values, beliefs, customs and "common sense" which support the outer cultural behaviors are under the water, and like the lower depths of the ocean, these areas are not often visited. Rather, they are simply taken for granted by those who are part of the culture, since they grow up in it, while those who are unfamiliar with the culture are generally unaware of these depths. These submerged components of culture include, but are not limited to our:

- Religious beliefs
- Morals
- Values
- Ideals
- History

These underlying elements that drive our behaviors come from a variety of sources and commonly we don't consciously think about them during our everyday business or personal activities. We are so steeped in our own culture, it is like an invisible shield guiding us. In fact, many of us pay little attention to where these underlying beliefs, values, and other inner characteristics come from and how powerfully they influence our behaviors. But our culture is there, within us and surrounding us. It is inescapable. It is as much a part of us as our physical form, and it is part of what makes each of us unique.

Gradually, what happens is that we are immersed in our culture and learn it as we grow up and interact with others in daily life. This culture is both the social environment we experience each day and the complete body of social knowledge passed on from generation to generation.

Thus, we learn culture from many different sources using different methods, all of which are culturally driven, whether we learn this information when we are children, or now as adults, formally or informally. These sources of culture include:

- Parents
- Family members
- Neighborhood and community members
- Educational institutions
- Social institutions
- Religious institutions
- The media
- Written documentation
- Observation of others in our own culture
- Historic legends and stories

These cultural forces influence virtually everything we do. They help us form our beliefs, thoughts, and how we act as individuals and as members of a group. That group of people then creates the culture in which it resides, whether it is in a remote village, a youth group or a corporation.

Yet, we rarely think about these influences. Just take a moment to realize this for yourself. How often do you think each day about the language you speak, the actions you take, the material items you value, or your attitude toward others? If you're like most people, not very often. Yet, when we come into contact with a person or group of people from a different culture, we are often reminded—sometimes even shocked into awareness—by our owns values, beliefs, and likes or dislikes. In fact, we often get an even stronger awakening when we come into contact with people who do or say things which run against what we consider "common sense," so we may immediately consider them *strange* at best, or dishonest or *rude* at worst.

But in reality, when we have this reaction, we are commonly experiencing an emotional cultural barrier, so that we are interpreting a behavior from our own cultural lens or prism, while the other person is acting out of his or her own cultural framework.

Another way to look at this process is to identify two people who are interacting as the *sender* and the *receiver*. The *sender* is the person who is choosing the words to speak or write, choosing the tone of voice or speed of the message, and choosing the body language or actions that go along with the message. The sender packages the message to accurately convey his/her meaning or *intention*. The *receiver* is the one observing and reacting to the behaviors, words, tones or speed of message as packaged by the sender. The reaction the receiver has to the sender is the receiver's *perception*. The challenge in cross-cultural situations is that there is often a significant gap between the true intention of the sender and the perception of the receiver. Thus, the opportunities for miscommunication are huge; even though a sender can have positive intentions, the receiver's perception can be negative. For example, when you as the receiver think a behavior rude, too aggressive or over familiar, the other person who is the sender, may think he is simply being enthusiastic and friendly from his own cultural perspective.

Since it is inherently difficult for people with different cultural backgrounds to accurately interpret the intentions of each other, to have good communication, it is imperative they take the time to identify and clarify mutually acceptable "rules of engagement." Part of this process involves getting to know not only the iceberg of your cultural counterpart, but your own iceberg as well.

THE CULTURAL ICEBERG

As the iceberg shows, the words, tones, and actions on the surface evolve from our own values, beliefs, and common-sense notions of reality. So when we encounter someone of another culture, we usually judge their approach, ideas or style based on our own underlying values, beliefs, and common sense perceptions. But this can lead to tremendous mis-understanding between people from different cultures. As the iceberg metaphor illustrates, we may not be accurately assessing the positive intentions of our cultural counterparts, and they might misinterpret our positive intentions. There are two reasons for this:

- The parties involved in the interaction are often unaware of their own underlying values and common sense; they don't know their own icebergs.

- The parties involved in the interaction don't know the values and the common sense of their counterparts' icebergs.

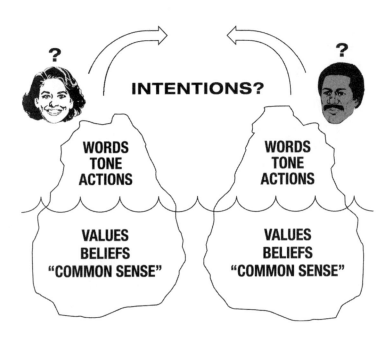

As a result, a common problem between people from different cultures is the tendency to mistake each other's behaviors, choice of words or tone as inappropriate or rude.

Thus, we need to work at developing a new sense, a "cultural sense" that transcends the "I'm right, you're wrong" approach and takes the needs and values of both cultures into account: for example, the needs you have as a business leader and the needs of your multinational customers and employees.

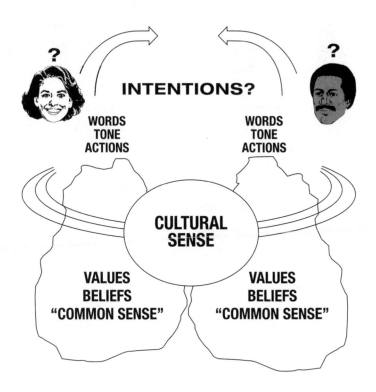

The problem illustrated by the iceberg is that you are relying on your own cultural premises of what is correct. By contrast, you will better understand and accept these differences, if you understand and accept the principles of intercultural effectiveness as a guideline.

PRINCIPLES OF INTERCULTURAL EFFECTIVENESS

- One culture is no more right, natural, or better than any other culture as long as it doesn't deprive a person from a different culture what they value.

Just because the people in one culture eat with their bare hands makes them no better or worse than those who choose to eat with wooden or metal utensils.

- All cultures have their own internal logic, and all behavior within that logic makes sense to the person from that culture.

The logic of "constructive confrontation" at Intel Corporation makes sense to them, because that is part of the corporate culture. However, the logic of "diplomatic differing" is common in many other corporations.

- Culture affects the attitudes/behaviors of many of the members, much of the time, but there are individual differences, so that culture plus individual personality determines behavior. Think about how inaccurate the following statements are:

"All southerners are the same." All northerners are the same." "All of those people are the same."

- Perception is selective, learned, and culturally determined.

We are the product of our upbringing. At Disneyland, the "Disney look" of short hair and no beards for men, and minimal makeup for women, is woven into the fabric of the corporate culture. That grooming standard is introduced when a prospective employee is interviewed, reinforced at new-hire orientation and supported by policy. It works for

Disney, but is not necessarily the best grooming standard for another industry, or another company with a different corporate culture, such as a software think tank in Silicon Valley or a surf shop in Florida.

- Withhold judgment. Inaccurate judgment and negative evaluation are among the biggest obstacles to intercultural effectiveness.

  Check with someone who knows the target culture, or a "culture coach," before jumping to conclusions (either positive or negative) about the behaviors you observe in cultural others. "The customers from XYZ culture are always negotiating for a better price. I don't like serving them." A culture coach might be able to offer effective strategies for interacting with people from that culture, for example: "Expect people from XYZ culture to ask for a better price. This is normal in their culture, so don't take it as a personal attack or as being rude. An effective response is to say 'thank you for asking, the price is as written in the advertisement', then continue with the sale."

- Cultural self-awareness and cultural other-awareness are critical tools for enhancing effectiveness.

  Get to know your own culturally determined likes and dislikes (your own iceberg) while studying the likes and dislikes of your multicultural customers and employees.

HOW TO DEAL WITH MEMBERS
OF DIFFERENT CULTURES

- Approach those from a different culture non-judgmentally, with a spirit of inquiry.

- Assume that differences exist until similarities are proven.

- Different cultures and different personalities require different approaches; be flexible, since no single strategy, tactic or procedure always works.

EXERCISE: THE EFFECT OF CULTURE
AND COMMON SENSE

The following exercise will help you recognize the extent to which culture is an influence, yet rarely thought about. It is divided into the following three steps and deals with an activity most of us engage in on a regular basis: the use of self-introductions to start relationships.

Step #1: Thinking about everyday introductions In your own culture.

Step #2: Thinking about everyday introductions with someone of a different culture.

Step #3: Thinking about how you learned your common sense about introductions.

STEP #1

Thinking about everyday introductions In your own culture.

Imagine you are meeting someone, in person, for the first time in a business situation. Close your eyes and see yourself where you conduct your business and think about how you would introduce yourself. What would you do and say?

Now, visualize what you expect from your business counterpart. What do you expect that person to do and say that send you the message of: "I'm credible," "I'm trustworthy" or "I am an honest person?"

Now, open your eyes and think about the images you have just seen. As you do, consider whether you really believe you have enough information to determine a person's character. You probably have made a snap judgment based on very little information. Yet, we do it all the time. In a typical North American environment, we generally expect the following as a minimum to judge a person we meet for the first time:

- A firm handshake
- Direct eye contact
- Both parties standing

In addition, we like it when our counterpart repeats our name and greets us with a salutation such as "Nice to meet you" or "How do you do," just as we might expect to do the same in greeting the other person. But we don't spend a lot of time with small talk. We like to get to the point of the meeting, then save the chitchat for after the task has been accomplished.

STEP #2

Thinking About Everyday Introductions With Someone Of A Different Culture

Now, take the same scenario of meeting a business counterpart for the first time. Again, close your eyes, so you can see the scene in your mind. But this time, imagine your counterpart does not behave as you expect. Rather, when you extend your hand, he merely puts his hand out, does not return your squeeze, and gives you a weak, "limp fish" handshake. Worse, he does not look you in the eye and speaks so softly that it is hard to hear him.

Now, notice how you feel about what you have just seen. Do you feel uncomfortable? Do you think the person lacks confidence? What else did you notice and experience, because the person didn't act as you expected?

Now, open your eyes and think about what happened. This experience helps to show how you might react when someone from a different culture acts in ways that don't meet your expectations. For most people raised in North America or for those accustomed to typical business greetings here, this kind of weak, unassertive greeting could be a complete turnoff, because of how we perceive these behaviors from our own perspective. We might even choose not to do business with such a person due to our perception of his lack of presence or insecurity, although in some other cultures, notably in Asia, what we consider a weak greeting is a sign of appropriate humility and respect.

These differences, even in an everyday greeting, show how culture influences us. Based on how we have been raised, we all develop a sense of right and wrong that becomes our common-sense guide for survival. If one or more of these components of expected behavior is missing—especially the direct eye contact and firm handshake—we tend to jump to negative conclusions about a person's character, integrity or honesty.

When we come into contact with people who have a different common sense and it comes out in behaviors that we don't understand or like, it is easy to criticize them and label them negatively. Often we don't think that this different behavior has validity, because it is not our own. But that's because most of us take our own approach for granted and don't think about when or how we developed it, such as where we learned the "proper" way to greet people and start business relationships. Do you know where you learned yours?

By contrast, a more constructive approach that will help you better understand and get along with people from different cultures is to assume that common sense does not exist across cultural boundaries. Assume that we have different underlying values, beliefs, and common sense perceptions, reflected in different behaviors, until you learn differently.

STEP #3

Thinking About How You Learned Your Common Sense About Introductions

Now, for the final step of this exercise, think about the number of times you shake hands during the day, whether in a business setting or on your personal time. Then ask yourself these questions: How often do you shake hands?

Where are you when you shake hands? Does your style

of shaking change depending upon the situation, person, or time of day?

Now, ask yourself the following questions: *How old were you and who taught you the "correct" way to shake hands the first time?* Can you remember where you were or why you were being taught to shake hands? You very likely cannot, because most people don't remember this.

Next, think about the components of a "good" handshake. How did you learn them? To distinguish the different components, ask yourself these questions:

- How hard do you squeeze your counterpart's hand?
- How many times do you "pump" your arm?
- How long do you maintain eye contact?
- Do you shake hands with one hand or do you grasp your counterpart's forearm or hand with your free hand?

The point of this exercise is not to reinforce a common behavior or to suggest one behavior is correct and the other, incorrect. It is merely to illustrate most of us go through our daily activities without ever thinking of why we do certain things. As long as the people we come into contact with behave as we expect and we behave as they expect, we will have fewer problems interacting. This is because: A) We either share the same cultural background; or, B) We have adapted to each other and made appropriate adjustments.

CULTURAL ADAPTATION

As the globe continues shrinking and we increasingly come

into contact with people from different cultures and backgrounds, the odds are high we will interact with customers or co-workers who don't necessarily understand or even value our common sense or behaviors. Cultural insensitivity stems from the belief that "*what's good for me is good for you, and if I like it, so should you.*" Unfortunately, that kind of approach is what leads to cultural miscommunications and misunderstandings. As a result, the companies and leaders that survive and thrive in the 21st century will be those who recognize, and then act, upon the following fundamentals for success:

- The values held so dearly as "common sense" by one culture are not universal.
- Behaviors common to one culture are not necessarily accepted by another.

What can be done to recognize these? And, once recognized, what kind of adjustments need to be made? Well, the list is virtually limitless, but at a minimum, you must assess how *flexible* or *inflexible* your current approach is. A more *flexible* approach or practice means you take into account the needs of your employees and customers who are foreign born or represent minority cultures. A more *inflexible* approach would suggest you have a set standard or method, (which may be have been very successful over the years) but are unwilling to change it. Areas to assess could include your product line, marketing strategies, personnel policies, management style, return policies, foreign language proficiency of employees, signage on your property and website design.

During your assessment, it is important to remember that

any adjustments or cultural compromises you choose to make represent a way of finding a bridge between icebergs through seeking a mutually acceptable "cultural sense" instead of a potentially divisive "common sense" approach.

USING STYLE SWITCHING
TO ADAPT TO CULTURAL DIFFERENCES

To make your product or approach more culturally appropriate, you can make adjustments by using an approach called *style switching*. This is the process of identifying differences in the values or beliefs of the customers, employees, or anyone else you are trying to appeal or relate to, then changing your product or approach accordingly. You change your behaviors—the way you communicate or interact with these people, not your basic values or beliefs. How? Here are some basic techniques and examples of how to apply this method.

To understand how style switching works, refer back to the Cultural Iceberg model. As you see, the people represented by the two icebergs each have unique and different behaviors and values. Neither side is right or wrong; they are just different. Now let's say that the woman by the iceberg on the left represents culture "A," and works for the company providing a service or product. Imagine that the man by the iceberg on the right represents culture "B," and is buying the service or product. Unfortunately, if the woman representing culture A in the iceberg model does not alter her approach, she could easily miscommunicate information or offend the man representing culture B.

This kind of model applies to the company as a whole, not just to individuals. Let's say that culture "A" is a world-renowned theme park called Disneyland, while culture "B" represents its many Japanese customers who visit the park (or "guests," as Disneyland prefers to call them). At Disney, when I worked there, and today, too, one of the most fundamental long-time corporate values is providing outstanding customer service. From the first day they start working at Disney, the concept of *"every guest is a VIP"* is reinforced on a daily basis. Employees are taught to always treat every guest with respect regardless of the time of day, how crowded the park is, or who the customer was.

However, even with the best of intentions, maintaining this value with the *appropriate* behaviors can be a huge challenge, as the Disney employees found. A big problem in the 80s was how to maintain great levels of customer service to *all* who visited our park, including the throngs of Japanese visitors. There were so many that a serious problem occurred at the Main Street shops every afternoon around 3:00 p.m. This is when hordes of Japanese tourists converged on the stores to purchase merchandise. As the Japanese pushed into the stores, many cut in lines to grab merchandise and then pushed to the front of lines to get to a register. Making the problem worse, none of the employees could speak Japanese, so the clerks at the registers didn't know how to talk to the customers they and their non-Japanese customers perceived as "pushy tourists." Also, the clerks didn't realize that this seemingly pushy Japanese behavior was due to some very basic differences between the Japanese and American cultures. You can see the differences most clearly, if they are lined up side by side.

JAPANESE CULTURE

1. The Japanese like to travel in groups and rely on public transportation. In California, they took tour buses to and from the park. The buses left the park every day at 4:00 P.M., so there was a mad dash at the end of the day to finish shopping.

2. The Japanese are obligated to purchase gifts to bestow upon friends and family members, upon return to Japan.

3. The "personal space" of the Japanese is much less than that of most Americans. They live in very crowded conditions and are used to being elbow to elbow with people all day.

4. The Japanese aren't used to waiting in lines, (crowded subways). Their attitude is that if you wait, you lose, so you push to front of the line.

AMERICAN CULTURE

1. Americans prefer to travel more independently in smaller groups and generally rely upon personal and rental cars. As a result, they can come and go according to their own schedules.

2. Most Americans do not feel an obligation to purchase gifts for friends or family members, although they may buy gifts for others as well as souvenirs for themselves.

3. The "personal space" of Americans is much larger than the Japanese. They live in more spread out conditions and are used to being farther apart from people when they stand and talk.

4. Americans have traditionally waited in lines.

As this comparison illustrates, there are major cultural differences. And how do you treat *every guest as a VIP* if the special treatment one group of customers only serves to alienate another group? In this case, the key to resolving the problem was not to judge one set of values or behaviors as good or bad. Rather, to solve the dilemma, Disney sought to find a way to maintain its value of customer service for all and think of a creative way to serve its Japanese visitors.

Eventually, the customer service department found two key changes that resolved the conflict.

1. Disney hired more English/Japanese bilingual employees and assigned them to the busiest stores during the busiest periods of the day. These employees staffed the registers and worked the floor to help the guests find merchandise.

2. Disney created roped-off lines or queues leading up to the registers and instructed the clerks to guide the guests into these lines.

These approaches might seem very simple, yet getting the strategies approved required a lot of work. First, the customer service department had to justify the cost of hiring more staff. Next, the employees had to develop and produce a new training program for the bilingual staff, resulting in higher costs. However, the improved customer service and sales justified this extra cost and effort. Both the Japanese and non-Japanese guests had a much better experience in the stores, and the clerks in the store felt much less stress.

Thus, Disney had to change its operating procedures, but it preserved its core value of customer service. In fact, making the change helped Disney maintain this core value, by providing even better service. In other words, Disney *style switched* to respond to customers with different cultural values and behaviors, and by doing so was able to create a mutually acceptable environment for Japanese and non-Japanese guests, and the Disney employees themselves.

RECOGNIZING CORPORATE CULTURE

As the previous example illustrates, it's imperative for any organization to know the cultures of its customers. It's equally important to get to know the style or culture of your own organization, since the corporate culture is a combination of what your company values and how it conducts business. Whether you are aware of your particular culture or not, you have one, since all organizations develop their own culture by design or default. An agreement about what is appropriate corporate behavior develops over time, and some organizations are more committed to—even fanatical about—developing and maintaining their unique culture.

The corporate culture of a company is reflected in any number of behaviors, including how meetings are run, the way e-mail messages are composed, and how direct or indirect, formal or informal, employees are with each other. Corporate culture also encompasses your dress code, work hours, and even what employees do after work and the extent to which they socialize with other employees or outsiders. Regardless of your particular corporate culture, a critical variable for success is how flexible it is and whether you provide room for change or style switching.

HOW EVEN LITTLE THINGS
CAN CREATE CULTURAL CONFLICTS

Example #1
The Disney "Name Badge Incident"

The importance of being sensitive and adapting to cultural

differences is even shown in some of the seemingly minor clashes, such as the "name badge incident," which occurred when Disney's corporate culture clashed with the Japanese way of doing things. Although what happened appeared to be a minor problem, it exposed deep cultural conflicts, and reflects the kind of basic issues that can create havoc in the global marketplace.

No one is immune from this kind of conflict and it can become even more prevalent as a company's corporate culture becomes more defined. Disney, even though it prides itself on service excellence and not making mistakes, still has a certain arrogance that runs through the corporation. This arrogance is a product of many years of success, and its certainty about its own knowledge of how to do things correctly. Unfortunately, that same certainty got in the way of its good relationships with others, particularly those from other cultures. Disney's "our way is the best way" attitude was particularly evident during the late 70s and early 80s, when the company was negotiating with a Japanese corporation, the Oriental Land Company, to jointly develop and build the first international Disney theme park. Though the park was eventually built as Tokyo Disneyland, there were many cultural bumps while building it, from the initial negotiations to construction and park operations.

To be fair, Disney is not the first company, nor the last, to have trouble with a foreign partner during such a large project. And when the Oriental Land Company initially approached Disney with the deal to build a theme park in Japan, their request was to recreate, to the last detail, the Disneyland found in Anaheim, California. Hence, the stage was set. Disney was in the driver's seat and the Japanese had requested a little slice of California in Tokyo, right? Unfortunately, the best intentions of both sides eroded into many bitterly contested arguments. Disney's renowned inflexibility, combined with the Japanese need to protect what they considered important, created an antagonistic environment that plagued the project from start to finish. This mutual resistance was never more evident than when the management teams of both companies clashed over the seemingly small issue of employee nametags, as ridiculous as this sounds.

But first, a little history lesson to clarify the passion of both sides is in order. With Disney, the problem goes back to a central principle which the company founder, Walt Disney, instituted from the earliest days of the company—using first names. He wanted everyone to be on a first name basis, including himself, and if anyone called him "Mr. Disney", he would often reply: "That's my father. Call me Walt." Thus, the tradition became established, and everyone at Disney referred to each other by their first names, regardless of title, age or length of time with the company—a common custom now, but revolutionary 45 years ago. Also, early on, Walt began the policy that all employees should wear little oval-shaped nametags with a Mickey Mouse imprinted at the top and, of course, the tag featured only the employee's first name. This was a non-negotiable pillar of the company's corporate culture and was a reflection of one of the most enduring American values: equality for all.

However, in the Japanese culture, as in many cultures of the world, it is commonplace to recognize and even promote social or professional hierarchical differences. This is done by showing restraint and by not becoming too familiar too quickly. The use of the first name is often reserved for one's closest friends or family members. Even then, when a hierarchy is present, it is highly unusual to use first names. In Germany, for example, colleagues who have worked together for years might still address each other by a title or professional degree such as "Doctor," but never by first name. The Japanese feel very strongly that using a first name is presumptuous, assumes equality and is even rude, especially in a business setting. In a culture that so reveres its elders, how dare a 25 year-old employee address his or her 50-year-old manager by his first name and not by his title or last name!

Unfortunately, neither the members of the Oriental Land Company nor the Disney team took any of this into account in the early stages of the negotiation. After all, why zero in on such mundane matters as cultural differences when discussions focusing on synergy, mutual benefit and the profits to be made are so much more fun!

Finally, the negotiations covering the details of the business relationship between the two companies were completed. The Disney team prepared to host, in California, a delegation of senior members of the Japanese team to celebrate the signing of the contract to create Tokyo Disneyland. In typical Disney fashion, the occasion was full of wonderful entertainment and the setting was perfect. When the Japanese executives entered the boardroom at Disney's headquarters, they found neatly prepared nametags for each of the visitors. However, the names on the tags were the first names of the Japanese executives, not their last.

As a result, the executives were shocked, for this was the first time they had ever seen their first names used in a business setting. Then, not realizing the Japanese viewed these tags as a personal slight, the American executives made the encounter even worse by inviting the Japanese team members to "join the Disney family by putting on your new nametags." Since the Japanese way is not to openly challenge a host, the Japanese executives reluctantly put on the tags, but their hesitation and expression of quiet dismay as they put them on made their displeasure very clear to Disney. It showed the Japanese felt very strongly it was inappropriate to use their first names and they needed to have their last names on the tags.

Incredibly, it actually took both companies six months to work out a resolution that was acceptable to both sides. Though it may sound surprising to quibble over such minute details, such minor differences can loom very large in cultural conflicts and are the source of many future business problems. In this case, the Japanese were adamant about keeping their last names on the tags, while the Disney executives were equally adamant about maintaining Walt's legacy of using a first-name basis. But something needed to be done to find a win-win solution that would consider the cultural needs of both groups and be a mutually acceptable solution for all. Both sides needed to style switch.

The eventual solution to this name-tag conflict was an ideal and logical mix of both cultures, though logic often doesn't prevail in these emotional cultural conflicts. But here logic won out when both sides engaged in some style switching to jointly create an ideal solution. The agreement was this: The Disney team and the Japanese executives agreed that while the Japanese were in the U.S. working at Disneyland as trainees, they would use a first name on their nametag, and they could use either their own name or a "westernized" version. Then, when they returned to Japan, they could use their last name on the tags at Tokyo

Disneyland. In coming to this agreement, both sides made what they considered a huge concession—giving up what each perceived as an essential long-standing cultural tradition, using first names for Disney, using last names for the Japanese—but the compromise was vital to ensure the success of the project.

Example #2
The DaimlerChrysler "Bathroom Sign Incident"

If the problems of nametags and theme parks seem ridiculous or far-fetched, let's take a look at the nuts and bolts industry of automobile manufacturing and what happened to Daimler-Benz AG and Chrysler when they merged. At the time of the merger, the relative strengths each company brought to the table were viewed as tremendous. Chrysler had been through extremely challenging financial times and emerged as a lean organization with much marketing prowess. In fact, based on money made from each car sold, it was considered the most profitable of the big three American car manufacturers. Daimler was known for its technology and impeccable quality. Daimler would help Chrysler crack the European market and Chrysler would lend creativity and speed to the sloth-like process Daimler used to develop new cars. Both companies would help the other expand in ways never before imagined; the two organizations, when merged, would be a working model of synergy.

Of course, this model of trans-global, intercultural effectiveness looked great on paper. Then the two cultures started working together. Like Disney, there were many problems, but one in particular reinforces the idea that the common sense of one culture is not always shared by other cultures.

As reported in the *Wall Street Journal*,[i] a fundamental of the Chrysler corporate culture was frugality. This was driven by Lee Iacocca, the man who negotiated the financial bailout of Chrysler by the U.S. government. Chrysler had been on the brink of bankruptcy, then fought its way back to become one of the most innovative and well-known car manufacturers in the world. On the other hand, the Daimler-Benz corporate culture wasn't based upon frugality but luxury. This isn't to say that Daimler didn't watch the bottom line, but just consider the vehicles they produced. Daimler is known for its luxury sedans, the cars of choice for an elite few. Chrysler fueled its comeback with the mini van, a car for the masses.

So, in spite the rosy predictions and best of intentions of both companies, the resolve of each was tested within a year of the merger. The price of the stock of the new company, DaimlerChrysler AG, plummeted. The reasons for the price erosion are numerous, with some attributable to the differences in management style between Germany and the United States. As the tension grew, one incident, in particular, seems to capture the essence of the differences.

A meeting to announce earnings was organized and held at a high-class New York hotel. An executive of the Daimler side of the business had authorized signs to be made that would guide visitors to the restrooms. The signs were created using the corporate colors of blue and silver and placed in a variety of locations around the hotel. Robert Eaton, who became co-chairman and co-CEO of DaimlerChrysler after the merger, saw the signs and is reported to have become incensed at the waste of money for something as unnecessary as bathroom signs. Given the brouhaha that erupted over this issue, one can only imagine the spirited, if not rancorous discussions that occurred when representatives from both cultures talked about new car designs!

Why on earth would a person in such a high position become upset about something as insignificant as bathroom signs? The answer is simple: The signs represented a dramatic departure from the corporate culture of the Chrysler that Eaton knew so well. The iceberg he had grown so comfortable with was changing as the Daimler and Chrysler cultures merged and the common sense of frugality at Chrysler was being threatened. This isn't to say that the culture of either corporation was good or bad. On the contrary, this story, as well as the Disney story, reinforce the idea that creating an effective hybrid culture that takes into account new ways of doing business can be traumatic.

So, whether creating nametags, bathroom signs, product lines or corporate strategies, it is important to take proactive steps to create an environment where thoughts and strategies contrary to the usual, monocultural ways of doing business are embraced, not dismissed.

BREAKING THE CULTURAL BARRIER

As these stories illustrate, the tendency of managers to dismiss the importance of dealing proactively with cultural differences and believing that "our way is the right way" is a major barrier to being effective in managing customer or employee relationships. Such differences are often dismissed by comments like: "There are really no differences. We are all striving for the same thing," or "Common sense is our best guide." But this head-in-the-sand attitude is a recipe for disaster in today's era of global commerce.

You have to know how to constructively deal with cultural differences and diversity to be competitive today. Merely accepting diversity in the workplace is not enough. Knowing how to adapt accordingly to cultural differences found in both your workforce and customer base can lead to numerous benefits. At a minimum, you can expect better teamwork and harmony with your internal customers, employees and co-workers. At a minimum, you should draw from a broader base of potential employees. In the proper environment, those employees could unleash their creativity to develop new products or ways in which to market and sell existing products. Also, you should examine your current and potential customer base and determine if there are unique ways expand both. If nothing else, you will benefit from having a better knowledge of your business practices and know if they are acceptable to the rapidly changing needs of employees and customers alike. If you do all of this with a vengeance, you could also enjoy increased productivity, greater leadership in the marketplace, and more sales and profits.

The following exercises will help you think about how aware you are to diversity issues in your own company and how willing you are to respond to make changes as necessary in your corporate culture or products and services you offer. They will help you better establish a baseline for assessing where you are now and where your customer service department or organization as a whole has to go to successfully break through the cultural barriers to success today.

EXERCISE #1

What's Your Customer Service Cultural IQ?

The following exercise is designed to make you aware of how good your customer service is—or isn't. While some of these questions can be applied to your customer service generally, they are also designed so you can think more specifically about how you respond to the special needs of customers, or employees, from diverse cultural backgrounds. First, see how many things you do that might be considered poor service and add up your score for that. The items which may be especially upsetting for customers from other cultural backgrounds—say, because they take an ordinary lack of customer care as even more insulting or demeaning than another customer might because they are sensitive to perceived racial or ethnic slights—are starred. Then, look at what you do that might be considered good service and add up that score.

Take the test individually and then you can combine your individual scores to get a group average—or simply compare and discuss them. As you go through the following questions, rate yourself, your department, and your company on a scale of 1 to 10, with 1 being very poor and 10 being outstanding service. Make copies of this scale so you can do these ratings separately. You can also do this exercise individually or as a group over time, say, every month or two, so you can compare how you or your group are doing.

SIGNS OF POOR SERVICE
DO YOU ANY OF THE FOLLOWING:

Show A General Lack Of Respect
- Don't treat all customers with respect.*
- Are too chatty or familiar with customer.*
- Don't really listen to customers, and instead give formula answers or excuses for why you don't do something or help.*
- Expect customer to understand and are unwilling to explain or help when they do not.*

Show A Lack Of Courtesy On The Phone
- Put the customer "on hold" and forget them.
- Transfer a customer without asking first whether it's OK to do this.
- Put a customer on hold without asking or waiting fo permission.

Show Feelings Of Frustration, Anxiety, Or Anger
- Show frustration and impatience in response to a customer's request.*
- Act or look frustrated.*
- Can't control your own temper or anxiety with a customer.*
- Act "put out" when a customer asks you for something.*
- Are openly hostile.*

Show A Lack Of Attention To Customers
- Keep a customer waiting a long time.*
- Ignore a customer.*
- Are too busy to answer questions.

• Are preoccupied with something else.

Blame Others Rather Than Not Blaming Anyone Or Accepting Responsibility Yourself

- Don't own the problem and blame someone else.*
- Don't apologize, even when you are wrong.*
- Make customer wrong.*
- Present yourself in a manner that suggests: "I'm the expert, who are you?"*

Show A Lack Of Commitment Or Follow-Up

- Make promises and then you break them or deny you made them.
- Don't follow-up on what you agreed to do or return calls to customers.

Inappropriately Give Priority To Customers

- Give priority to customers you like.*
- Serve the loud, obnoxious customers first before other less demanding customers.*

Show A Lack Of Initiative Or Preparation

- Wait for customer to approach them for help.*
- Don't anticipate needs.
- Not prepared.
- Unorganized.

Have Poor Conversational Or Language Skills

- Talk too fast/ Interrupt.*
- Talk too low/mumble words.*
- Use language inappropriate for situation.*

- Use obscene language.*

Poor Demeanor Or Unprofessional Appearance
- Don't smile.*
- Don't make eye contact when talking with someone.
- Act overly stiff and reserved, like a robot.
- Chew gum or eat while working.

Lack Of Knowledge Or Willingness To Find Out
- Say you "don't know" and you don't know something you should.
- Won't willingly get supervisor when you don't know or customer seeks more help.*

Lack Of Flexibility
- Unwilling to be flexible and brush customer requests off with, "That's the policy."*
- Respond to an unusual request with a comment like "I can't help" or "I can't do that."*

Showing A Lack Of Concern For Customers' Needs
- Send customer on "wild goose chase."
- Don't recognize previous customers, either by general recognition or by name.

Inappropriate Behavior With Other Employees
- Gossip with another employee.
- Don't coach or help new employees.*
- Talk poorly about company/department. in front of customer.

SIGNS OF GOOD SERVICE
DO YOU DO ANY OF THE FOLLOWING:

Treat Customers With Respect and Courtesy
- Treat all customers with dignity, respect.*
- Say "Thank you."
- Greet customers by their last name when you know them (Mr., Mrs., Sir, Ma'am).*

Show A Positive Attitude Of Care, Concern, And Helpfulness
- Act in a caring, concerned way.*
- Are friendly and positive.*
- Are patient and supportive.*
- Are sincere.*
- Smile.*
- Never say "no."
- Are available when needed.
- Are consistent in always showing these positive attitudes.

Have Initiative
- Initiate service.
- Anticipate needs.
- Surprise the customer with services not requested.

Provide Fast Service—Without Rushing The Customer
- Provide quick service, but don't rush the customer.
- Provide service quicker than customer requested.
- Don't hover over customer.

Knowledgeable And Provide Information
- Know your product.
- Find information when you don't have the answers.*
- Share the information you have about a product or service with the customer.
- Guide the customer through the process instead of "data dumping" through giving the customer handouts or details and expecting the customer to know what to do.*

Good At Follow-Up
- Provide follow-up.*
- Return calls promptly, even if only giving a status report, so the customer doesn't feel forgotten.*

Have Good Language And Communication Skills
- Use language appropriate to the situation.*
- Listen attentively.*
- Don't interrupt.*

Are Flexible To The Customer's Needs
- Can "read" needs of customer and adjust.*
- Flexible.*

Are Sensitive To The Customer's Point Of View And Give The Customer A Sense Of Control
- Put yourself in customer's shoes.*
- Offer options: let customer make the decision.*

Are Willing To Take Responsibility
- Problem ownership: "Don't pass the buck."
- Problem ownership: Don't send you to "next window"

for information, they find it for you.*
- Empowered to make decisions, don't always have to "call the supervisor."
- No excuses, just action.

Willing To Apologize For Mistakes
- Apologize, make customer "right."*
- Say "Sorry to have kept you waiting."*

Supportive Of Co-Workers
- Teamwork: Don't criticize other employees or departments in front of customer.

Now think about your answers to these two sets of questions. While many of these questions are mirror images of each other, they are designed to have you think about both what you do wrong and what you do right. Then, you can work on doing less wrong and more right, so as your score of wrong answers goes down, your score of what you do right will go up. To help you do this, ask yourself the following questions, so you can begin working on those behaviors you want to improve—and reminding yourself to keep doing—and feel good about doing—those behaviors you already do right.

What three behaviors would I most like to change? What can I do to change them?

Behaviors To Change

1._____

_____

2._____

_____

3._____

_____

What I Can Do To Change Them

1._____

_____

2._____

_____

3._____

_____

What three behaviors would I like to continue doing or do even better?

Behaviors I'm Doing Right

1._____

_____

2._____

_____

3._____

_____

What I Can Do To Make Them Even Better?

1._____

_____

2._____

3._____

_____

EXERCISE #2

Rating Your Team's Customer Service Approach To Customers From A Different Culture

Now that you thought about your individual customer service approach, think about how your team as a whole is doing. Do so as a group, and use this exercise to stimulate a dialogue and discussion. Choose one member of your group to act as the facilitator and another to write down the group responses. List all of the responses as in a brainstorming exercises, and then go through the list to rate the areas where you are the strongest and areas where you need to most improvement. You can use a group voting technique—like asking each person to use a rating scale from 0 (lowest) to 3 (highest); then add up the totals and divide by the number of members of the group to get a group mean. Finally, pick the 3 or 4 highest rates-effective areas and improvement areas. Then, compliment yourselves for your achievements and get to work on making the improvements you have identified as a group.

Your Most Effective Areas	Group Rating
_____	_____
_____	_____
_____	_____
_____	_____

_____   _____
_____   _____
_____   _____
_____   _____
_____   _____
_____   _____
_____   _____
_____   _____
_____   _____

Your Areas for Improvement   **Group Rating**

_____   _____
_____   _____
_____   _____
_____   _____
_____   _____
_____   _____
_____   _____
_____   _____
_____   _____
_____   _____
_____   _____
_____   _____
_____   _____

[i] Ball, Jeffrey and Miller, Scott. "Stuttgart's Control Grows With Shakeup At Daimler." *The Wall Street Journal* Vol. 60, September 24 1999.

CHAPTER THREE

FROM "COMMON SENSE" TO "CULTURAL SENSE:" THE SIX MUST-KNOW OBSTACLES TO A GLOBAL SERVICE APPROACH AND HOW TO OVERCOME THEM

Sooner or later, all companies with a multicultural base of customers or have emplooyees who come from a variety of cultures run into problems. These problems are due to cultural differences and the inevitable misunderstandings and miscommunication. These problems are especially perplexing when you first start on the journey to transform your company into a global service company. After all, in spite of your best efforts to become more attentive to a diverse set of needs, the odds are great you will make mistakes that have the potential to drive away some of your customers and employees who come from diverse cultural backgrounds. The key to resolving these problems, or avoiding them in the first place, is to learn in advance when and where such problems typically arise, rather than *after* the mistakes are made, as many companies do. Why not take the initiative in avoiding fairly predictable problems?

The core cause of many of these problems is that a vast number of companies still operate as though their customers and employees came from one common background or culture. There are six, very predictable, incorrect approaches companies use because they are following their traditional (and largely ineffective) *common sense* approach to customer service and management, rather than the more appropriate *cultural sense* as described in the previous chapter. If they were to use a more effective *cultural sense* approach in developing their business strategies, service philosophy, or management style, they would undoubtedly have a more successful business model, resulting in increased sales, market share, more loyal customers and employees.

So how does your own company measure up? Are you and your employees using a traditional but often outdated *common sense* approach where you deny cultural differences in your own dealings, or are you ready to make the full transformation from a locally focused to a globally focused company where you recognize cultural differences and adjust your policies, procedures, and products or services accordingly?

The six major problem areas or issues to resolve are the following, and I'll be describing what to do about each in this chapter. They are:

1) Failing To Apply The "When In Rome Factor."
This is a fundamental for cross-cultural effectiveness and sets the stage for resolving the remaining five problem areas. This first area highlights the need for cultural flexibility and adaptability.

2) The Time Factor: Or, Are We Looking At The Same Calendar?

This issue underlines the need to address different senses of time to ensure good relationship building.

3) Language, The Great Equalizer Fallacy.

This highlights the issues and differences that even learning a foreign language doesn't overcome.

4) The "Are We Really That Different?" question.

This debunks the argument that tries to deny cultural differences and invites certain failure.

5) The "Happy Family" Cover-Up.

Which seeks to ignore observable differences by stressing only similarities, and invites failure, too.

6) The "One Size Fits All" Team Building Approach.

Which assumes that a team successful in one cultural context will be successful anywhere.

To fully examine these issues, each of them is divided into the two subheadings of "Common Sense" and "Cultural Sense." Common mistakes made due to cultural ignorance or arrogance will be highlighted under the "Common Sense" heading. In contrast, the more culturally appropriate attitudes and behaviors will be introduced under "Cultural Sense."

At the end of the chapter, you'll find several exercises and worksheets to help you assess how your company rates on each of these six problem areas—whether you are more *common sense* or *cultural sense* oriented, and what can you do to increase your cultural sense, in designing and implementing your policies, procedures, products, and services.

But first, in order to effectively change your approach from the problem-ridden attitude of *common sense* to the more effective, *cultural sense* approach in each of these areas, you need to understand and be able to use a technique that's called "style switching," briefly noted in the previous chapter. This approach attunes you to both your own cultural style and that of others, so you can better change, as appropriate, between styles with people from different cultural backgrounds—a technique that's especially vital when you want to personally relate to or introduce a product or service to an intercultural or international audience. This way, by switching styles, you can operate from your *cultural sense* rather than your *common sense* and be more effective.

So how do you get the knowledge? One key way is to trust those who know the buying habits, service demands or expectations of your multicultural customer and employee base and use them as coaches. Although it is often difficult to feel trust toward those outside your cultural group or organization in these super-competitive times, you need to develop trust in those with the cultural knowledge, so you can use them as "coaches" to help guide you through the inevitable maze of questions and problems. While this book can help you gain an increased cultural awareness and know how to generally apply it in a wide variety of situations, you still need some help from these "cultural insiders," in the know in your particular area, because every community of people from different cultures can have widely differing needs and you have to be able to act accordingly.

The process is much like what happens when an

anthropologist goes into a new cultural community to do a study and looks for an informant as a kind of mentor or guide to help the anthropologist gain entry and acceptance and learn the basic fundamentals about what's acceptable behavior and language. Then, as the anthropologist gains this crucial initial acceptance, he or she continues to learn from others in the culture about what to do, thereby refining the process of learning how to interact. This process is vital to learning not only what to do, but sometimes even more critically, what not to do, so as not to break any deeply held taboos, or simple social conventions. People may not only be deeply offended, but they could end the entire interaction or even ask you to end any further contact with the group if you do.

Likewise, in a customer service context, you have to be aware of the cultural do's and don't's of a particular group, and often the only way to know this is to receive guidance from someone who is either already inside or well acquainted with the culture. Thus, to get this information, ask the advice of those who know your target audience—or better, are actually part of it—then act upon that advice. Amazingly, a large number of companies either don't ask for or ignore this advice, commonly because of three major reasons:

- **Ignorance:** They just don't know. (They say: "Gee, I didn't know"!)

- **Arrogance:** They don't feel the need to learn. (They say: "We have been very successful in the past, so we don't want to mess with a good thing."

- **Lack of Trust:** They don't think someone else knows. (They say: "Who are you—or who is any outsider to tell us how to run our business?")

This kind of organizational myopia is very much in contrast to the way individuals commonly look to experts in a wide variety of situations in learning something new, such as a new sport or new subject in school. For example, most people planning a first-time whitewater rafting trip for a vacation would look for advice from friends, travel agencies, and wilderness guides because they had never been on a raft before. They would want to know how to ride on a raft, what to take on the trip, how to keep from falling off, and the like. In fact, many would want a whitewater rafting company to plan the trip, including setting the menu, providing experienced guides, selecting the kinds of boats to safely make the trip, and choosing the rivers and where to run the rapids. And then the guides would be the ones actually steering the raft and making the minute-by-minute and day-to-day decisions about how to proceed.

Most people would want to set up this trip this way, because they prefer to put their experience in the hands of seasoned professionals. It just makes sense to do so, because these are the ones with the knowledge we need to have a good, safe trip—which is exactly the opposite of the ignorant, arrogant, lack of trust approach that many companies use in dealing with people from other cultures. Or more specifically, our reasons for seeking out the knowledge of professionals in this rafting context are the following:

- **Education:** We realize they have the knowledge we need, since as we collect information for our vacation, we come to recognize how complex and potentially dangerous a rafting vacation can be. So we want to become more informed and less ignorant to have a fun, safe trip.

- **No Arrogance:** We know we are beginners and don't have preconceived notions of what a competent job involves. So we don't attempt to tell them how to do their job. How can we. We don't know, and know we don't necessarily want to know.

- **Trust:** We are willing to trust these professionals and follow their advice, because we have done our homework to learn who the experienced, reputable guides are and we have chosen a whitewater company or rafting guide based on recommendations from sources we trusted, whether friends, books, or a community good service ratings guide.

Thus, when it comes to dealing with people from other cultures, you have to be ready to style switch and look to those people who are in the know about that culture. In fact, you might think of the people who know the unique needs and customs of your targeted customers as like your whitewater rafting guides. They know how to help you speed ahead quickly and safely through the river, because they can help you maneuver past obstacles and can offer advice about the product, service or policies you are considering introducing or changing. But instead of calling them guides, you might think of them as a valued *culture coaches* whose advice you should consider before you make any decisions on policy or product issues.

You should turn to such a guide and trust this advice, because a culture coach is a person or group of people, who represent or know the cultural group you are appealing to. Or perhaps for even greater assurance, you might initially get advice from a number of culture coaches before deciding which one or ones to rely upon before making any decisions. The reason for listening to these multiple viewpoints is because everyone—including members of the culture you want to learn about—has personal biases and prejudices, which will influence how he or she looks at issues and other people. So culture coaches who are younger or older, male or female, from one city or another, and so on, will have somewhat different experiences and perceptions about the same culture. They all will be valid and more knowledgeable than your own, yet different—much like members of different generations in our own culture have different views on issues ranging from leadership or management style and "good customer service" to entertainment and fashion trends. Thus, it is a good idea to get feedback from culture coaches representing different segments of a group you are trying to appeal to, such as: women, men, older customers or employees and younger customers and employees.

So where do you find these culture coaches? In any number of places. You can find them in your own company among employees or managers with different cultural backgrounds or experiences, and outside your company in community groups. You can also set up a formal program to gain the knowledge of outside cultures through customer focus groups, led either by someone in your company or organized for you by a market research firm, ad agency, or other professional organization that sets up these panels.

However you proceed in trying to contact a coach and get information, the most important thing to remember is that you don't have all of the answers. Instead, look to these culture coaches as your link to how to best interact with your multicultural customers and employees, so you can successfully use style switching in your personal interactions and in the kinds of products and services you introduce into different cultural markets. To this end, you should rely on the advice of these coaches, then combine their insights about culture with what you already know about your business, core competencies, and markets to develop a *cultural sense* approach based upon the information you have gained. In this way, you will be able to effectively use this more enlightened *cultural sense* approach rather than the insensitive and failure-prone *common sense* approach many companies still rely upon today.

And now, with that backdrop about the approach to use, here are the six key issues where it is especially important to use this approach to effectively relate to your customers and make decisions about what products and services to introduce and how.

THE SIX MUST-KNOW OBSTACLES TO A GLOBAL SERVICE APPROACH AND HOW TO OVERCOME THEM

#1) Failing To Apply The "When in Rome Factor"

You've probably heard the phrase: "When in Rome, do as the Romans do." In use since before the Middle Ages, it a derivative of the proverb "*When you are in Rome live in the*

Roman style; when you are elsewhere live as they live elsewhere," which is credited to Saint Ambrose, who lived from A.D. 340-397. It is now commonly used to suggest when you go someplace different, it's good to adapt to local customs, like when you're traveling to a foreign country.

Likewise, in a business setting, it means that if you're going to do business in a foreign culture or domestically serving people from another country, it's a good idea to act or relate to them in a style they find familiar and comfortable. In other words, applying the "When In Rome Factor" is another way to say we must adapt our products, policies and service standards to be successful in a global environment. It means using your *cultural sense* rather than your *common sense* to do the right thing. In spite of the long history of this proverb and the obvious message for intercultural effectiveness, there are numerous examples of individuals and companies who fail to apply the message.

For example, here's what an employee relating to customers from a different culture might think under these two conditions:

USING "COMMON SENSE"	USING "CULTURAL SENSE"
"I'll just be myself and they will know that I'm sincere."	"It feels strange to do business this way, but since I know the benefits, I'll do it."
(But unfortunately, when you're yourself, they won't think any such thing. They may think you are being rude, insulting, or simply clueless—not sincere!)	(Yes, that's the ticket. And even if you don't get it exactly right, they'll appreciate the effort and respect for their culture, and maybe they'll even help you get it right the next time.)

Unfortunately, many companies ignore this fundamental rule of success for conducting business in a foreign environment or domestically with multicultural customers, resulting in misunderstandings, offended customers, lost sales, and other problems. But if you apply your *cultural sense*, you'll have a better chance of style switching, to help you to act more effectively—"when in Rome"—that is, when you are in another place or relating to a customer from another culture. As previously noted, style switching means altering a product, service, approach, or organizational strategy, though you still can preserve your underlying mission, values, and beliefs. That way you stay in tune with your customer—not only paying attention to needs and desires, but the "how" of successfully satisfying those wants and needs.

You want to make this shift, since you can't assume your multicultural customers or employees will be satisfied with the products or services you have historically relied upon, even if they have been successful in the past, because customers now are more culturally sensitive and demanding. In today's global age, customers simply have more choices, plus customers from different culture are waking up to their increased power—either because of increased numbers (such as the growing Hispanic community in the U.S.) or because of growing technical sophistication. Plus, a growing music, film, and media explosion of multicultural products are bringing that message home, too—that expressing your own culture is cool and having it recognized is even better!

Thus, especially now, you need to recognize the benefits of altering your product line or service policies to adapt to the cultural groups you serve. This means reassessing any long-held *common sense* rules of conducting business to determine if they are outmoded or inflexible, then evolving to the more modern global or *cultural sense* perspective, which has the needed flexibility to serve your multicultural customers or employees in the way they want to be served and understood.

Certainly, as in any personal or corporate style switching, you may experience an often predictable hurdle of feeling discomfort, even confusion and pain, when this new approach contradicts what you have always held to be "right," "correct," "natural," or just the "company's traditional way of doing business." As the previously described nametag incident at Tokyo Disneyland illustrates, it was very difficult for Disney employees to put aside their old *common sense* notions that Disney's decades-old first-name policy was the right way to go. It took six months of fighting with Japanese counterparts before the American customer service employees agreed to style switch based on what the managers and employees in Japan wanted— because in effect the American–based Disney was now in Rome, even if it was called Tokyo. So what made cultural, not common sense, was to "do as is done in Rome."

#2) The Time Factor:
Or, Are We Looking At The Same Calendar?

The next big area where you need to adjust culturally is in your sense of timing, since the value of time varies widely from culture to culture. Different values regarding the use of time are at the core of much frustration when multicultural groups work together. Typically, the individuals from a culture with a slower time sense feel pressured, while those from the faster time-oriented culture feel impatient and frustrated with delays.

This is particularly a problem for U.S. companies, since we value the efficient use of time so much. Our ideal is to do everything as quickly as possible to get the most out of every day. Compared to many cultures around the world, we are literally obsessed with time and efficiency. For examples, we use words like "timely," one of our most popular magazines is called "*TIME*®," we have round-the-clock news casting with the latest news, and any number of books and training seminars devoted to the topic of time management. Plus, with the ever-expanding use of the internet and e-mail, many companies now operate 24 hours a day on "Internet time," which has sped us up even more.

Yet, while our goal may be to make the most *"efficient use of time"*, the word *"efficient"* is laden with values. It implies it is good to be fast and quick in accomplishing a task, which is what we consider efficient. But what an American sees as efficient could be viewed by a person from a different country as impatient, rushed, and rude, and thus not efficient as all, since they are assessing what's efficient from a different standard. To them, efficient might mean do what you can to have a good, warm, trusting, friendly relationship. Thus, relying upon our ordinary *common sense* to set time schedules or assess how efficient our cultural counterparts are is a prescription for misunderstandings and cultural clashes.

For example, here's a typical situation in an office where using *common sense* doesn't work while using your *cultural sense* does—getting a customer to commit to a proposal. In this case, here are two possible reactions a sales manager might have:

USING "COMMON SENSE"	USING "CULTURAL SENSE"
"They should have responded to the proposal by now. Do they really want to do business with us?"	"I wonder if we should follow up or continue waiting? I better check with my cultural buddy to find out the reason for the delay and what to do."
(Maybe they do and it's just taking them longer, because they are operating under a less urgent time-line. Or if they don't, maybe it's because they feel under too much pressure from you to meet your faster time schedule, or you haven't taken the time to establish a solid relationship based on their values.)	(Yes, that's exactly what to do. If you don't know, check with someone who does, so you can find out how they are proceeding and what you might need to do differently...from their perspective.)

Unfortunately, when you don't take this different cultural time-sense into perspective, you can fail to make the sale or create other problems, such as happened when a major American company tried to expand its market share overseas without taking into account the cultural values of both the local salesforce and customer base. Faced with pressures from headquarters to implement an efficient sales strategy, the company departed from its strategy of using independent sales agents, who had actually done a good job representing the company. In fact, in one particular product line, the company enjoyed a 90 percent market share. It helped, of course, that the quality of a similar product from their primary local competitor paled in comparison to the well-designed U.S. product. Eager to capture more market share, the company decided to hire their own local sales staff and train them in the more efficient sales strategies that had been so successful in the U.S. market. In most cases, the independent sales agents chose not to join the company as employees, so a new sales team was hired.

After hiring the local sales staff and training them in the United States, the company began to pressure its field sales associates to act to quickly and aggressively, using that as a measure of efficiency, rather than setting its policies and measures according to culturally based benchmarks of how to approach the sale. This approach was driven by executives who had little or no experience in the target country. The company, a well-established producer and marketer of quality personal care products, had a great reputation and high level of success in the United States. Like any organization, the company had developed its own corporate culture, which included a high value on advertising and selling its products. And not surprisingly, in keeping with this value, the company's executive ranks were filled with men and women who had come up through the advertising and sales divisions, so they brought with them into the executive suite those U.S.-centric ideals of to sell and promote products.

But then, the company ran into trouble when its flawed expansion of its sales force in Asia. Determined to achieve quick successes with this market, the company sent a management team from its advertising and sales divisions to devise a market penetration plan. However, rather than listen to the advice of the employees they hired in that country, they relied upon the *common sense* they had developed through selling products successfully in the U.S. Under that formula, the sales staff was supposed to make at least 16 sales calls per day to the retail stores selling their products and then quickly show the buyer their product line, resulting in an average a sales call lasting about less than 10 minutes.

This recipe worked in the U.S. because the store managers here had a similar common sense measure of efficiency, so they didn't want to spend time with the salesperson. They judged themselves effective by the same standard of making a quick profitable buy for the store, so during a typical sales call, they would lead the sales rep to the shelves where the merchandise they had previously bought was stocked. Then, the sales rep would quickly check the stock on the shelves and in the storeroom, and inform the store manager of how large an order to place to refresh the inventory to its previous level. It was a process that allowed the sales rep to move quickly and efficiently from store to store, and it relieved the store manager of the burden of constantly tracking the stock—so it was a win-win arrangement for both. But it worked in the United States because of the high value on time, expressed in the phrase: *"Time is money,"* which is exactly what it did. It provided for the maximum number of calls in the shortest period of time, which made more money for everyone in the transaction—the sales person, the store manager, and their respective companies.

However, while this approach worked well in the U. S. where speed is valued more than nurturing interpersonal relationships, it does not work well in places where interpersonal relationships are much more highly valued—which is the case in many other countries.

Unfortunately, this company tried to operate in its business-as-usual mode, based on its 16 sales call a day model, but the market it was trying to penetrate was in a country where human relations came first before business. The independent sales agents the company had used in the past knew this, and combined with a superior product, had built a strong market. As a result, the retail store managers wanted to first connect on a personal level with any new sales reps before discussing business. They felt it necessary to do so in order to establish that feeling of trust and rapport they required to do business. For them, a sales rep was like a neighbor or distant family member, and they had to have the relationship established on a strong basis first before they were ready to do business.

Yet, driven by its past domestic success, the company ignored the advice of it's locally hired staff, who tried to explain about the local differences and the importance of putting personal relationships first. Instead, the top execs simply handed down their order by fiat that regardless of local conditions the sales reps should continue to carry out 16-calls-per-day to keep their job.

And so the sales reps did- if they stayed with the company—but with disastrous results. Of course, while the American company was embarking on this "efficient" sales approach, its main competitor in Asia was busy improving the quality of their product. So, armed with a much improved product and the strong personal ties to the store owners due to their more traditional sales techniques, the Asian competitor stole the lion's share of the market.

Within one year, the American company's share of the market, once a mind-boggling 90 percent, dropped by more than 50 percent, and its turnover of key sales personnel zoomed to an all-time high, compared to a much lower level of sales turnover in the U.S.

#3) Language, The Great Equalizer Fallacy
Another big area where there are cultural myths and misconceptions is in the area of language. The common prob-

lem here is thinking that once people are speaking the same langauge, they are *speaking the same language*. What this means is that while people may outwardly be using the same words, phrases, grammar or body language, they may use this language with very different meanings. Not only does this occur within the same language group in different regions of the country, but it occurs in different socioeconomic, racial, and ethnic groups (i.e., in Oakland, California, the school board even attempted to create a bilingual track based on what some people called "eubonics" or black English). And then, there are even more differences when you have people from a different country who have learned a foreign language.

Thus, you can see where the typical example of using your *common sense* to think that everyone speaking English is saying the same thing can go horribly wrong, and you need to apply your *cultural sense* to really understand what someone is telling you—and to recognize how they may not always understand you, so you have to be very clear and clarify that the other person really knows what you said and meant. It is equally important for those Americans who speak a foreign language, (a terribly small percentage of the population) that knowledge of the words alone does not guarantee success. A knowledge of the culture behind the words, and the body language that accompanies the words, is equally important.

For example, here are two typical situations where using your *common sense* can get you into linguistic hot water, while your *cultural sense* could provide just the right temperature for good communication.

USING "COMMON SENSE"	USING "CULTURAL SENSE"
Thinking Linguistic Fluency / Cultural Fluency	Realizing Linguistic Fluency / Cultural Fluency
1) "They speak English (or I speak their language), so we should have no problem communicating and getting the job done."	1) "They speak English (or I speak their language), but they may not use the same words or have the same meanings, so I should be extra careful to make sure we both understand each other."
2) "He nodded his head in agreement, so that means he understands and supports what I asked him to do." (But unfortnately, this kind of attitude will contribute to actually having problems in communicating and getting the job done.)	2) "Well, he did nod his head during the meeting, and it looks like he understood what I said, but I don't know him well enough to assume he understands or supports my request. I'll check with one of my colleagues who also attended the meeting and who knows him very well. Perhaps he can help interpret the behavior". (Exactly. Because of these differences in language usage that may not be immediately apparent, that's why it's crucial to clarify understandings.)

Such language problems can be reflected in many different ways. For instance, if you try to translate something into another language, you can easily run afoul of differences in meanings, including even when you try to use a popular name or brand in one culture and find it doesn't have the same meaning or even an opposite meaning. A classic example is when Chevrolet tried to introduce it's Chevy Nova automobile into Latin America and was surprised it wasn't selling very well. Why? Because in Spanish, the word "Nova" translates into "No va" which means "No go"—not the name you want for a reliable source of transportation.

In addition, body language can be a huge source of frustration and miscommunication. When does the nodding of one's head mean "I agree with you", versus "I am sending merely you the message that I'm just awake and listening?" When does the absence of words, silence, actually mean "I have no opinion on that subject, so please continue," versus "I am violently opposed to that idea, but because of my respect for heirarchy and my inability to debate effectively in your language, I will hold my tongue"?

Let's take a look at how the use of a language by someone from another culture can easily conceal differences in values. There are two great examples from my days in Japan during the period leading up to the grand opening of Tokyo Disneyland. As with any grand opening, the list of things left to accomplish before opening day was far lengthier than the time left. Hence, the atmosphere was ripe for miscommunication.

THE CASE OF THE "CLEAN" HAUNTED MANSION

What does the word "clean" actually mean? This might sound like a simple question, but a lack of clarity about this word led to a problem that cost tens of thousands of dollars to remedy. In March 1983, the grand opening of Tokyo Disneyland was less than one month away. As a way to prepare the Japanese staff for the rigors of actual operations, a series of "soft openings" was scheduled. These soft openings were for a limited number of invited customers such as the media and other VIPs, hence the potential for positive publicity before the public grand opening was tremendous. As such, the pressure to put on a good show for this select audience was equally tremendous.

The night before the first soft opening led to the first disaster. One of the American managers spent the evening extolling his team of Japanese custodians and housekeepers, who worked the night shift, to be extra meticulous when cleaning the stores, restaurants and rides. "Make this place shine!," he said, in a final motivational burst. True to form, the Japanese staff set out to do as ordered. They cleaned the park as it never had been cleaned before.

I think the call to me came at about 7:00 a.m. "They cleaned the Haunted Mansion, they cleaned the Haunted Mansion"! he screamed. "Isn't that what you reinforced in your little pep talk last night?," I asked. "Yes, but I never imagined they would clean the Haunted Mansion *completely*!" "So, what is the problem with that?," I asked. "I'll tell you what the problem is, they cleaned all of the cobwebs, wallpaper stains and dust that the artists so meticulously created to make the place look haunted!," he complained. He was furious that no one had clarified what the word "clean" meant. "They just all nodded their heads while I was speaking, and I was using an interpreter, so I assumed they understood what I wanted them to do." My ensuing cultural explanation fell on deaf ears. I explained that in the Japanese culture, the subordinate rarely, if ever, will question the orders of a superior. This is particularly true in a public forum, such as when the American manager gave his pep talk. "Why, that's stupid, back in the United States, my staff would immediately question my directive if it made no sense to them," he exclaimed. Well, it is pretty obvious that this manager was operating from his set of common sense rules and never took the time to clarify the rules his Japanese staff was following. Language was only part of the problem in this case. Odds are that the same crisis would have occurred, even if the American manager spoke perfect Japanese.

ICE SKATING, ANYONE?

This second situation also occurred during the period of soft openings before the official grand opening at Tokyo Disneyland. Equally amusing in hindsight, it was a major catastrophe at the time. An American operations manager received an emergency call in the middle of the night from his Japanese supervisor of operations. The Japanese supervisor was quite agitated because a late season snow storm was dumping more snow than the groundskeeping crew could clear. They had used every available crew member to run snow blowers and actually resorted to trying push brooms; anything to clear the snow that was rapidly building up on the streets and sidewalks of the park. Realizing there were only a limited number of hours left to take care of the situation, the American manager told his supervisor to "wash the snow off the streets and sidewalks." When the Japanese supervisor asked the manager how he proposed they do it, the manager replied, "Use the fire hoses, melt the snow, then wash it into the street drainage system." He issued this mandate at 2:00 a.m. By 4:00 a.m., they had a beautiful sheet of ice covering the areas of the street and sidewalk that had been washed down. Needless to say, that area of the park had to be roped off until the ice melted later in the day.

This was definitely not a case of a language blunder. The

Japanese supervisor understood perfectly what the American manager had said. In fact, the Japanese supervisor spoke flawless English. He had even attended an intensive, six-month, on-the-job training program at Disneyland in California to learn the ropes of park operations. Yet, even though he recognized his manager's directive was flawed, he didn't push back during the telephone conversation. The reason? The American manager was so abrupt and impatient. When I interviewed the American manager years after the incident, he was able to laugh at the whole scenario. As he said during an interview I conducted, "Yeah, I was out of my mind with so many details to take care of before the grand opening. Plus, he called me in the middle of the night, so I wasn't exactly at the top of my game and I know I came across as 'I'm the boss, do as I say.' To be honest, I didn't know what to do, so I just blurted out what I thought would take care of the problem. Look, I was born and raised in southern California, so what do I know about snow removal? I sure wish he had told me I was crazy, but he merely said 'I understand.'"

The common sense of the Japanese was that it wasn't his place to question what his boss said, especially when the boss was so directive and upset. The common sense of the American was that an American employee, who recognized the negative consequences of what could happen, would have so advised his manager. Language wasn't the issue; the culprit was that the two of them hadn't developed a mutually agreed-upon set of ground rules for interaction. There was no cultural sense. Thus, as these stories illustrate, it's crucial to pay attention to the way you are using language with someone of a different culture and how the meanings you intend with your words are being interpreted by someone else. Or conversely, be aware that you may not understand correctly what someone else is telling you and be ready to ask questions to clarify what you are unsure about or may not understand.

#4) The "Are We Really That Different?" Question?

Another major source of intercultural conflict is ignoring or trying to cover up cultural differences by believing you and your cultural counterpart share like goals or have the same attitude towards interpersonal and business relationships. A method often employed to defend this wrong-headed approach is to use the argument of human nature, which espouses we are all underneath basically the same. While there is some truth to the notion that there are common qualities that make us human, this kind of myopia overlooks the wide degree of variation due to socialization and life in different cultural settings. There is no way to accurately reduce down to a one-size-fits-all orientation the individual behaviors, goals, ideals, priorities, or the many other characteristics that make us unique. As discussed in the previous chapter, we are each a mixture of characteristics coming from a wide variety of sources, like a layer cake of variation, due to personality, social class, age, gender, neighborhood, parenting, region—and on top of this is additional variation introduced by culture.

Such differences are why using the "common sense" argument to deny differences makes absolutely no sense. For instance, here's what the "common sense" thinker might say, versus the person who shows the perceptiveness and curiosity of the person who shows good "cultural sense."

USING "COMMON SENSE"	USING "CULTURAL SENSE"
"There is no such thing as a cultural difference. We're all humans with the same goals. So there's no need to do another employee survey. We've already done it and gotten the answers here."	"How do they give feedback? Do they focus on the positive or on the negative? Are they more cooperative or independent in their attitudes? Are they willing to take more initiative or would they prefer stronger leadership? How and when do they use humor? There are so many potential differences. Let's ask them so we can find out what the real story is."
(But unfortunately, if you don't ask the right questions, you'll get the wrong or inaccurate answers. And just because one group answers one way, another group could answer the same questions very differently.)	(That's right. You don't know. So you need to ask.)

Very often companies fail to recognize these differences, because they feel the pressure of standarizing and simplifying in today's fast-moving global age. They want to systematize and streamline, and are seeking economies of scale through uniformity, formalized guidelines, company-wide policies and procedures, common employee guidelines, and the like. Such an approach might work fairly well in the case of mainstream American culture and even cover over a range of personality, social, and regional differences. However, because of commonly held values and goals, such as being pragmatic, independent, taking initiative, being optimistic, and the like, this approach might be ineffective, even generate quiet unexpressed hostility in an environment that's quite different.

For example, in the U.S., an employee incentive program to promote better customer service based on employees competing against each other for the award of the week might work quite well, since Americans tend to like competition and enjoy the race to be the best. But such a rewards program might simply make employees uncomfortable and undermine morale in another culture, such as among some people from the Middle East, Latin America or Asia, where the emphasis on being cooperative and showing humility could make the competition a de-motivating experience.

Similarly, different cultural environments can produce very different attitudes toward life and work, even within the same country *or company*. For example, a style of meeting that worked well in a factory environment might *not* work well at the headquarters of the same company. Or, a style that worked well in New York City could possibly backfire in Minneapolis or Charleston, simply because the different cultures contribute to a different orientation to life. And even emotional feelings and reactions differ from culture to culture, from the more buttoned-down, controlled, hold-it-in approach of cultures like British and German, to the more emotional and expressive cultures of southern Europe, particularly in Italy and France.

In short, if you are going to be working in the customer service area, you need to be especially attuned to the vast range of differences in cultural traits that influence individual personality traits or other characteristics that relate to class, gender, age, neighborhood, region, and other factors. Though there may be some common qualities due to human nature and some shared goals, the cultural differences are far vaster. So you need to pay attention to these differences, and where you don't know or aren't sure, be sure to ask.

#5) The "Happy Family" Cover-Up
A fifth cultural error is an all too common off-shoot of problem

number four. It is the result of ignoring cultural differences. This error is embracing the myth of the "Happy Family" school of thought. Except in this case, you believe regardless of any general cultural differences amongst your employees, those differences won't matter because you are "all one big happy family." You believe being part of a corporate family is enough to overcome any cultural differences, and you want to ignore or paper over any differences because you think any focus on cultural differences will drive a wedge between people, not bring them together. So, why deal with diversity if you can ignore it? Remember the "Disney name badge incident" from the first chapter? This was a classic example of ignoring cultural differences in the name of maintaining family unity, a decidedly flawed approach. Of course, if the approach was to focus solely upon differences, you could create the environment where employees are left wondering: "I know the differences between my common sense approach and the common sense of my colleagues and customers, but how do we bridge those differences to build a stronger relationship?"

USING "COMMON SENSE"	USING "CULTURAL SENSE"
"Focusing on differences will only serve to drive us apart."	"We need to start by understanding the differences and similarities, since that's the first step to developing mutually acceptable goals, standards, and strategies."

To create a truly "happy family," it is important to focus on three areas: 1) The differences, 2) The similarities and, 3)

Mutually acceptable approaches to fill any gaps between numbers one and two. While the intention is good, a similarities-only approach can actually create a negative environment for employees. "Why doesn't my manager care about my opinion?" "Why doesn't the company recognize the unique needs of people from my culture and adjust some of the policies?" Of course, a company cannot bend to the unique needs of every culture represented in the employee group; there has to be some sort of corporate culture that is steady and predictable.

The key is developing a *mutually acceptable* set of policies, procedures or approaches that meets the needs of both the company and the employees, a strong corporate culture that transcends individual personalities or idiosyncracies. A corporate culture that reflects cultural sensitivity will then be the bedrock of a truly diverse "happy family." With this in place, a company or organization should work doubly hard to employ and train people who fit into that culture and be proud to invite them into the family. On the flip side, once the culture and direction of the organization are set, there should be no remorse in letting go of people who no longer "fit." The company should be increasingly discerning as its culture develops. There is no need to be whip-sawed by the myriad demands of a diverse set of employees. If the corporate culture already reflects multicultural sensitivity, the company should not feel compelled to jump in a million directions to satisfy the needs of a self-centered few. A strong culture will also simplify the hiring process; people who fit will stand out and people who don't fit will stand out, so it makes decisions about who to invite into the family much easier.

Though your goals may be admirable in wanting to create a "why can't we all get along happy family," the failure to address differences can easily push these differences under the table. Yet, they are still there and will eventually fester, causing problems when these differences suddenly appear front and center and can no longer be ignored.

Ironically, what seems counterintuitive in the heads of those who want to sweep cultural issues under the rug, namely exposing differences and similarities, is exactly what needs to be done. The focus on differences and similarities, then strategies to bridge those, is what can help bring company members together, while efforts to create a false unity can actually create divisions and conflicts that drive people apart—so the results can be opposite to what you might expect. For example, discussing the different expectations that employees from different cultures have about how to conduct or receive performance reviews could uncover vital information about how to improve the process. This doesn't necessarily mean changing the company policy about the overall compensation plan, but it could mean changing how a manager chooses to structure the review session itself. More specific detail about how managers can style switch is covered in chapter six. Thus, the lesson here is to use your cultural sense to create a truly happy, *diverse* family, to achieve more effective, harmonious results, whatever your cultural mix in the company and customer base.

#6: The "One Size Fits All" Team Building Approach
The final big issue that can interfere with developing a good cultural sense is the "building a team" dilemma. This is based

on making inferences from the past successes of a particular group to think that same group will be effective in the future under other circumstances. This is similar to the belief in the power of the track record and tradition that keeps many companies basking in past successes and failing to innovate, with the result they don't respond to change and they lose out in the marketplace as new changes pass them buy.

The same kind of head-in-the-past thinking can affect customer service, leading to a false evaluation of how a team will perform in the future based on past performance. In fact, exactly those same qualities that have contributed to a successful performance, such as a keen insight into the local or regional market, may mean that the team will not be successful when their new task is putting in place the same agenda in another cultural setting. What worked so well in Boston, may not play equally well in Beijing. So you need to think more culturally and globally about what will work in a different cultural setting or how to go after local customers who have a different cultural background. While some former team members will do just fine and can bring an expertise based on their own skills and past experience in carrying out the work of the team, you usually need to bring in some team members who have some personal ties or more hands-on experience with this different culture. This way you create a multicultural team that has the advantage of both past experience and an understanding of the new conditions the team will face.

An example of the differences in this approach is shown below, where the one division leader is using a past "common sense" approach to team building, while the other has the more realistic future oriented "cultural sense" approach that leads to success.

USING "COMMON SENSE"	USING "CULTURAL SENSE"
"I'll put my best team on this project. They have been very successful on similar projects domestically."	"I want to put together a new team that has the best in technical or task expertise and also understands the culture. Maybe I could get a few team members who know how to do the tasks plus some new team members who know the target culture."
(But unfortunately, that domestic success is not what it takes to make the project work in a different cultural setting, and your best team may be blinded by its past success from doing what's needed in the new project.)	(Yes, exactly. You want to combine a Technical Expertise, or Task Knowledge, with a Cultural Sense, or Process Knowledge, which is the key that equals Success.)

Thus, at a time when there is a growing popularity of cross-functional teams, you want to think about making these cross-cultural teams as well. You want to mix both technical expertise, drawing on people from different divisions as needed (such as combining people with a marketing, sales, and customer service perspective) with different cultural knowledge to provide even better customer service, because you will better know your customer.

A great example of building a team that can adjust to cultural differences comes from E*TRADE Financial. Founded nearly 20 years ago to provide online quote and securities services trading information, it has steadily evolved over the years. From its humble beginnings as a discount all-electronic brokerage, the company has reinvented and grown itself into a global leader in personal financial services with branded websites in the United States and several countries around the world.

Part of their success is their ability to rapidly adapt to

constant change, an invaluable quality given their profession! "In addition to providing outstanding service, simplicity and savings to our customers, one of our fundamental values is timeliness and speed," states Connie Dotson, chief communications and knowledge officer at E*TRADE Financial. "We have survived in a constantly changing environment by being able to attend to the needs of both our customers and associates. With that said, we don't rush into projects without thinking through them," Dotson states. She reinforces this approach with the following example: "For example, when we developed a new website for our Chinese market, we were careful to put together a team of more than 20 Cantonese and Mandarin-speaking experts to ensure our design was culturally appropriate. One-third of this team was already on staff and we brought the rest on board to complete the team. Combined with our local staff, we wanted to be sure to cover all of the cultural and business bases."

It is clear that E*TRADE Financial has taken the steps to create a multinational team that effectively reflects local needs and corporate values, a true "cultural sense" approach.

FROM COMMON SENSE TO CULTURAL SENSE: IT'S UP TO YOU

By analyzing the six areas introduced and analyzed in this chapter, you have experienced some of the most commonly occurring challenges facing organizations today in the global marketplace. At this point, the importance and benefits of transforming the culture of an organization, or the style of a leader, from the old-school common sense to the more global cultural sense should be abundantly clear. The organizations that will succeed are those, both large or small and with or without international operations, who remember the importance of becoming more aware of, and responsive to, cultural differences. Why not learn from the mistakes and successes of others, as introduced here, to assess your own approach?

Remember, these six keys are:

- The *When In Rome Factor*—Adapting to local customs, even at home.

- The *Using The Right Timing Factor*—Being aware of the time sense of others.

- The realization that *Language Is Not The Universal Equalizer* because meanings differ.

- The recognition that even though we are all humans, *Differences Really Are Differences*, and they cannot be ignored.

- The reminder that we *Can't Pretend We Are All One Happy Family* and expect team membership to cover over cultural differences.

- The knowledge that *Successful Teams Blend Technical And Cultural Expertise* and merely following the "one size fits all" is a recipe for failure.

So with these key areas in mind, how would you assess your organization, team or department? Do you tend to apply *common sense* or do you more often utilize *cultural sense* with your internal and external customer relations?

EXERCISE #1

Your Customer Service Approach: How Do You Rate?
Now in light of your understanding of differences about customers from different cultures, think about how both you and your whole team are working together to better satisfy these customers. Ask yourself the following questions, and perhaps do this as a group exercise, where you discuss these questions with your team. Ask these questions for each cultural group of customers you serve, and notice if there are any differences in how you are relating to these different groups. This will give you a sense of your flexibility and adaptability.

- What are you and your team doing that is working?
- In what areas can you and your team improve?

After you ask each question, use the space below to list your strengths and areas for development for each cultural group. Use a separate sheet for each group of customers.

Customer Cultural Group:_____

Effective Areas: (Behaviors, Attitudes, Work Environment)

_____

_____

_____

_____

_____

_____

_____

_____

Improvement Areas: (Ineffective Behaviors, Attitudes, Work Environment)

_____

_____

_____

_____

_____

_____

_____

_____

_____

_____

EXERCISE #2

Creating The Customer Response Matrix: What Constitutes Good and Poor Service For Different Cultures? Here is another way to look at how your service appears to your foreign-born and locally born customers. As in the previous exercise, it is helpful to engage people from the target cultures or at least people who have a good understanding of the culture. This can be done with focus groups of your customers and/or your employees. Just fill in what you consider the major differences as you think about your answers in the previous two situations of customers responding to poor and excellent service.

NATURE OF SERVICE

	POOR SERVICE	GOOD SERVICE
FROM U.S. CULTURE		
FROM A DIFFERENT CULTURE (SPECIFY)		

TYPE OF CUSTOMER

CHAPTER FOUR

FROM 'LOCAL SERVICE" TO "GLOBAL SERVICE:" SUCCESS STORIES FROM COMPANIES THAT HAVE BEEN THERE

What does it take to succeed in this expanding global market? How do companies adjust to the needs of a multicultural customer base and workforce? Is it worth all the trouble? These are compelling questions that are not easily answered. Yet, models of success exist.

The premise of this book is that any company, large or small, can reap tremendous benefits by catering to a culturally diverse customer and employee base. To reinforce this concept, this chapter introduces actual case studies of companies that have gone through the process of transforming a local service or product into one that is attractive to both local and international customer alike. The issues range from simply translating instruction brochures into other languages, to completely altering a product line or a business philosophy. The case studies introduce five well-known companies, highlighted below, that represent a wide variety of fields, from resorts and retail to transportation and manufacturers of industrial-grade machinery.

The companies, from large to small and representing a variety of industries are:

- **Continental Airlines**: This airline has gone "from worst to first" in customer satisfaction in the last five years and is a pioneer in providing innovative service across cultures.

- **FMC FoodTech**: Two subsidiaries of the FMC FoodTech family, **FrigoScandia** and **Stein**, which are world-leaders in the fields of industrial freezers and equipment that processes convenience foods.

- **The Pebble Beach Company**: The internationally renowned premier golf resort.

- **Northstar-At-Tahoe**: Ranked as one of the Top Ten Family Ski Resorts in North America.

- **Starbucks Corporation**: Pioneer of the coffee house and specialty coffees, it transformed a commodity product into international success.

Consider the following three points when reading these case studies:

- Learn through the experience of others that even the major multinational companies are not above making mistakes, and what they did about it.

- Consider the variety of strategies, large and small, for creating an environment of global service to both customers and employees.

- Assess the effectiveness of your own approach with your multinational customer and employee base.

CONTINENTAL AIRLINES: THE RE-BIRTH OF A CORPORATION

"Diversity is no longer a politically correct 'program' or another word for affirmative action. We are living in the most diverse society in history and our workforce and our customers reflect that diversity," states Pat Bissonnet, director of diversity for Continental Airlines. "Our goal is to create an inclusive work culture where everyone is treated with dignity and respect." Bissonnet knows the challenges many organizations face when hiring, then retaining, good employees. "We know the importance of recruiting employees, yet we also recognize the need to create a welcoming culture for our employees, regardless of their background." Continental is aggressively and successfully addressing a topic that has eluded many organizations: how to make the culture of the organization a welcome one for employees and customers who come from a variety of cultural, ethnic, linguistic and lifestyle backgrounds.

Have they been successful? You bet. "Employees are constantly telling me how much they appreciate the steps we have taken to create a corporate culture that stresses working together and treating both employees and customers with dignity and respect," says Pete Garcia, vice president of sales and marketing for Latin America. "Some companies institute diversity programs and do just enough to get by from a legal perspective. Not us. Working together is the basis for our global and domestic success. It is much like a good marriage, the more you understand your partner and they understand you, the better."

For the critics out there who question the potential bottom line impact of such initiatives, consider this. In 1997, Garcia's department launched a new initiative, the Latinization Program, to improve Continental's presence in its long-standing Latin American market. The results are impressive. Revenue from this market topped $1 billion in 2001, a four-fold increase in revenue from Latin American countries in four years.

From Worst to First—The Rebirth Of A Corporation

It is no secret that Continental Airlines has seen its share of tough times. On the ropes in 1995, it has made a meteoric rise to success in the last six years. In fact, Continental's chairman and CEO, Gordon Bethune, has written a book entitled: *From Worst To First: Behind The Scenes Of Continental's Remarkable Comeback.* Bethune's book chronicles the airline's rise from bankruptcy to an award-winning, profitable company known for its top-notch customer-service and reliable performance.

But this remarkable improvement isn't the result of the superficial and largely ineffective approach taken by so many organizations. The so-called "organizational change" in many corporations needing a new approach is usually nothing more than an anemic attempt to change the color of the paint on the wall. Many companies simply put up motivational posters, recruit employees from top schools or competitors, or roll out any number of initiatives or programs, without ever changing the true fabric of the corporate culture. Instead of changing the color of the paint on the wall, Bethune and his team first tore down the walls. The folks at Continental Airlines have succeeded through dogged, hard work and an unparalleled recognition that the customers and employees of today and the future are far more diverse than ever before.

Working Together: The New Corporate Culture

For the sixth straight year, Continental is operating under an operational imperative known as the *Go Forward Plan*. This is the airline's blueprint for success and drives virtually every aspect of the business. Comprised of four components they refer to as cornerstones, this plan is much more than the obligatory vision or mission so often found, and ignored, in many organizations, large and small. The four components of the plan are labeled: Fly To Win, Fund The Future, Make Reliability A Reality, and Working Together.

As you read the descriptions of the following cornerstones, you will find language describing financial, operational and strategic philosophies that are remarkably benign. In fact, you might find yourself thinking, "what's so special?" Indeed, no small number of organizations have their own version of Continental's Go Forward Plan. They just call it something else, such as their mission or vision statement, or operation principles, or any number of other catchy names. There are two very important differences to recognize between Continental's plan and the approach so often used. The first difference is to note that Continental elevates the human resources function to a "Cabinet level" of importance by including it in the cornerstone identified as *Working Together*. The second difference is that Continental practices what it preaches. Since its inception in 1995, every aspect of Continental's business has been reflected in these four cornerstones and decisions are measured against each; they truly set the tone for the culture of the corporation.

Continental Airlines' Go Forward Plan

Fly To Win—This is the cornerstone of the marketing division and helps them focus their efforts so as to achieve top-quartile industry profit margins. Part of the strategy for growing the airline is to expand international-airline alliances and continue eliminating non-value-added costs.

Fund The Future—This is the cornerstone of the finance division and focuses on the standard areas of reducing interest expense, and developing existing assets.

Make Reliability A Reality—This is the operations division cornerstone and the one most visible to Continental's customers. It focuses on having an industry-leading product the employees of Continental are proud to sell. Specifically, to rank among the top of the airline industry in the four key U.S. Department of Transportation measurements: on-time arrivals, baggage handling, complaints and involuntary denied boardings. This reminds all employees to keep polishing the company's image and constantly improve the product.

Working Together—This next one is the key to Continental's success in this era of global customer service and is the focus of this entire book. This is the cornerstone of the human resources division and starts with the statement: *Have a company where employees enjoy coming to work every day and are valued for their contributions.* Other statements include: Treat each other with dignity and respect. Focus on safety. Make employee programs easy to use. Keep improving communication. Pay compensation that is fair to employees and fair to the company.

Cultural Adaptability The Continental Way

So what does Continental do that sets it apart from so many other companies? Let's focus on the cornerstones from the operations and human resources divisions, *Make Reliability A Reality*, and *Working Together*, respectively, to get a clearer picture.

I. Make Reliability A Reality: The Latinization Program

Within the cornerstone of *Make Reliability A Reality* is the goal of ranking among the top of the airline industry in the four key Department of Transportation measurements: on-time arrivals, baggage handling, complaints and involuntary denied boardings. Let's visit one of the four, complaints. The obvious solution to achieving this goal is to have the fewest possible complaints and Continental has taken some extraordinary steps in this area that exemplify the concept stated in the subtitle of this book: *"From Local Service To Global Service."* Let's take a look at four of those steps:

#1: Cultural Awareness Training: As mentioned above, Continental embarked on its Latinization Program in 1997. Hoping to expand a market in which it was already successful, Continental took a multi-pronged approach to expanding its presence in that market. One of the first things on the to-do list was to raise the awareness of its employees about the countries and cultures of the region. Recognizing that, as Pete Garcia says: "not everyone from Latin America drinks tequila or dances the Samba," was a critical learning point. To address this, Continental developed a training program in 1996 called the "Seven Wonders Of The World." This program was designed to make employees aware of the different values they would meet based on cultural expectations. The program was provided to agents who worked on the front lines and who would interact directly with customers. The Seven Wonders program proved to be so successful, that a second-generation program called "Capture The Power Of Diversity" was created in the summer of 2001. This program reinforces Continental's philosophy of striving to understand the diverse cultures of its employees and customers, then meeting their needs with dignity and respect. It accomplishes this by defining cultural and diversity concepts and the positive value of diversity in the workplace. The course is a combination of skill building and self-awareness and challenges the participants to identify ways to create opportunities for providing the best customer service in the industry. The target audience for this program includes domestic and international airport agents, supervisors, team leaders and station management. In essence, it is a training program that emphasizes the importance of, and gives specific guidance on how to provide great customer service in a multicultural environment.

"As providers of service, we need to recognize that the cost of an airline ticket for some of our global customers could represent a considerable amount of their savings," Bissonnet says. "However, that same ticket might not represent nearly the same financial burden for U.S. domestic business traveler who flies on a regular basis. Our customers from overseas can have varying expectations of good service. We have to be sensitive to the value they place on money. How does it compare to ours? What do these passengers consider as normal regarding carry-on baggage? We must also be sensitive to the value various cultures place on the concept of time and be able to expedite the boarding process without coming across as pushy."

Through this training program, participants are exposed to some of the most fundamental, culturally driven issues that they could face when interacting with their global customers. Employees are much more effective and empathetic if they understand the culturally driven nature of values and behavior. Being aware that the customer could have a very different idea of what constitutes good or bad service, and knowing what to do about it, is a tremendous benefit for any employee.

#2: Ask The Customer: "As part of our Latinization Program, we gathered data from our customers to help determine where we needed to make changes," says Garcia. So Continental created a customer service questionnaire that asked two fundamental questions. "We asked our customers what they liked about the U.S. airlines they had flown and what they liked about the Latin American airlines," he says. The data from the responses showed that they liked the safety and reliability of the U.S. carriers and the personalized service, Spanish-speaking employees and hot meals of the Latin American airlines. This data drove the changes listed in the next two items.

#3: Alter The Product Line: "We have a group of professional chefs that we call our 'Congress of chefs' who are continuously creating in-flight meals that will appeal to a wide variety of tastes," says Garcia. "For our Latinization Program, we needed to determine what meals would be acceptable to passengers from Mexico, Brazil, Puerto Rico, Costa Rica as well as the United States. We run taste tests with employees as well as passengers to ensure we are providing a product they will enjoy." In addition to altering the menu, Continental changed the time the meals are served - lunch at 3 p.m. and dinner at 8 p.m.

#4: Staff Accordingly: Citing another finding from the questionnaire, Garcia says, "Many of our customers in Latin America are used to much more personalized service than what is common in the United States. Therefore, their expectations can be higher." In response, Continental hired close to 200 additional employees to help customers with flight connections, documentation and reservations. Even in airports where there is not as much traffic from Latin America, Continental added signs written in Spanish. "We put bilingual agents and employees wherever there are forks in the road, where a customer might need help," says Garcia.

The results of these efforts have been remarkable, to say the least. In the Mexican market alone, Continental now serves 20 cities. Five years ago it served only seven. "Outside the U.S., Mexico is our largest market, as measured in the number of cities served by our airline within a single country," says Garcia. In addition to the fourfold growth of passengers and revenue from the Latin American market, Continental has found success in other areas as well. With their focus on *respect* and *dignity* for all employees and customers, Continental is now enjoying a more satisfied and loyal domestic and international customer base and, more satisfied and loyal employees. It is a classic example of a win-win scenario.

II. Working Together: Taking Care Of Your Internal Customers, Your Employees

Continental's stated goal of ensuring all employees and customers are treated with *respect* and *dignity* is not merely a pretty statement that looks good in the annual report. It is a living, breathing part of their corporate culture that is reinforced on a regular basis. As mentioned earlier, the *Working Together* cornerstone is a guideline that affects virtually every business decision. Let's take a look at four, highly effective ways Continental brings life to one of the statements found in this cornerstone: "Make Employee Programs Easy To Use."

#1) Trust In The Good Judgment Of Employees: According to Bissonnet, "When we reorganized six years ago we eliminated a 600-page corporate policy and procedures manual and replaced it with the 67-page Working Together Guidelines. The Working Together Guidelines begin with one page of Working Together Expectations. We trusted in the good judgment of our employees to interpret these expectations appropriately, and we have not been disappointed."

#2) Flexibility Is The Key: Another statement from this cornerstone, *"Treat each other with dignity and respect,"* is found in one form or another in the policies or mission statements of virtually every major company. Valuing diversity is included as a "must have" statement in the corporate literature of many organizations, but in reality carries about as much weight or sincerity as the mechanical sounding "have a nice day" or "enjoy your meal" phrases we so often hear. Not at Continental Airlines, however. Continental has programs in place that elevate this concept of treating each other with dignity and respect and breathe life into it. One of Continental's corporate values is that employees should be able to ask any question and get a straight answer. Bethune holds employee meetings where employees can ask any question and get a straight answer. Every vice president holds similar meetings with those in their division. In addition, each corporate officer has a station he visits regularly, then acts as a liaison between his "local involvement" station and corporate headquarters. This direct link with even the most remote locations is unique to Continental and is a direct reflection of the statement, *treat each other with dignity and respect.*

#3: Communicate, Communicate, Communicate! Part of treating employees with dignity and respect is to keep them informed of current events in the company. And, true to form, Continental doesn't rely on just one method to get the message out. Continental uses a number of creative communication strategies to make sure it reaches its employees.

Among them are:

Continental Quarterly, a full-color newsletter sent out once per quarter directly to employees' homes; and Continental Times, a monthly, four-color newsletter. And, for those employees who don't seem to have the time to read,

Bethune broadcasts a weekly voice mail message that is sent out every Friday afternoon. Just to make sure all bases are covered, they even send out e-mail messages to employees, either at the employees' office computer or to their home computer, whichever is most convenient. Last but not least, every break room has one of two bulletin boards: either a good old-fashioned bulletin board or a high-tech LED electronic message board that has up to the minute news about stock prices, on-time percentage of flights or any other pertinent information.

#4: Involve And Educate: According to Bissonnet, "We live in one of the most diverse societies in America. One of the key goals of my department is to help make management aware of all of the dimensions of diversity and how they impact the way we manage. To address that, we have developed a new seminar for our leadership called 'Leading for Inclusion.' In this full day seminar participants look at the historical basis for change in America, and examine the data from the Census report, 2000. We engage in lively discussion of how to manage the changing workforce and use our diversity to achieve a competitive advantage." A common response from those who have participated in preliminary sessions is, "It is a real eye opener."

Like many companies, Continental has a harassment-prevention training program, but unlike many companies, Continental's program has a positive approach. Instead of focusing only on what employees shouldn't do, the program focuses on the Working Together expectation that everyone should be treated with dignity and respect. There is even a vignette that shows employees working together to heal the workplace after an issue has been directly confronted. This program was rolled out to all 51,000 employees, and enjoyed the solid support of management. As part of the proactive approach, front line managers introduced the program and set a positive tone by talking with employees about all of the ways their workgroup demonstrated dignity and respect for one another, and congratulated them on their successes. Managers also let employees know that their door is open to talk with employees about any conflict that they experience in the workplace. Given the positive, not punitive, nature of these workshops, the pattern at Continental is that people *want* to participate. Also, since *Working Together* is one of the four cornerstones of Continental's blueprint for success, employees and executive alike realize the direct connection between their participation in the workshops and their business success, a link that many companies fail to make.

Some Final Thoughts

A comment made to Bissonnet by an employee effectively sums up the feeling within Continental that their emphasis on dignity and respect is working. Bissonnet was visiting various employees to talk about their perception of how effective the company was in implementing Working Together. The company had just begun its on time arrival incentive program. The program was developed for employees at the manager level and below and has very clear goals: It pays monthly bonuses when the airline hits targets for on-time arrivals as scored by the U.S. Department of Transportation. Eligible employees receive a $100 bonus when Continental ranks first in on-time arrivals and a $65 bonus when the company ranks second or third, or achieves an on-time performance of 80 percent or better. Bissonnet was visiting a station where more than 50 ethnicities were represented in the employee group. She asked an employee whose job was loading baggage onto aircraft how well he and his fellow workers got along in this very diverse workgroup. He replied, "Look, it doesn't matter what color we are, what country we are from, or whether we are women or men; we all have the same goal of getting that bonus so we work as a team."

By the way, Continental started the performance bonus program in January 1995. It broke into the Department of Transportation top four ranking in February and to the number one position in March 1995. Pretty good for a company that had come in last in this same category in January 1994.

Is what Continental has achieved easy? Not if management and employee alike don't live and breathe and support the four cornerstones on a daily basis. Hard business decisions are driven by each component of the Go Forward Plan and sound human resources programs need to be in place to support these efforts. For example, the on-time performance bonus program cost Continental $2.5 million each month the $65 bonus was paid out. However, the cost of not being on time cost Continental $5 million each month. So the hard numbers supported the program which cut operating cost, resulted in higher employee motivation and created a more reliable product the customers wanted to buy. Every manager and employee knows that their future with the company rests, in part, on their efforts and accomplishments in meeting these goals and they are reflected in their annual performance reviews. Managers who know that their management style is not inclusive will seek out training so that they can improve their performance. "Quite frankly, if a manager can't lead through dignity and respect, Continental isn't the place for that manager," says Bissonnet.

In addition to the bottom-line benefits Continental has enjoyed, the initiatives of the past six years have resulted in numerous intangible benefits, such as creating a newfound pride in the organization; employees who enjoy working together; and people feeling included, regardless of their position in the company. If all this isn't enough, consider the fact that Continental was named one of the "100 Best Companies to Work for in America" by *Fortune* magazine for the third consecutive year in 2001.

Continental has proven that their strategy of Working Together is a sound business plan and, coupled with their global perspective, has resulted in tremendous domestic successes as well.

FMC FOODTECH: THE "TASTE" OF SUCCESS

If you have ever done one of the following, the odds are that the product you purchased or ate was processed by a piece of equipment developed and manufactured by FMC FoodTech, one of the many companies in the FMC Technologies family:

- Eaten a hamburger, chicken nuggets or french fries at a local fast food franchise or restaurant.

- Purchased frozen fish sticks or vegetables at the supermarket.

- Purchased frozen chicken in any processed form such as breaded nuggets or pre-cut portions.

FMC FoodTech is an operating group of the FMC Technologies Inc., which is headquartered in Chicago, IL, and represents more than 30 highly respected product brands. Within the FMC FoodTech family are companies that are world leaders in the field of the value-added processing of convenience foods. They manufacture, sell and service equipment and systems for portioning, batter-breading, cooking, frying, chilling, freezing and packaging of quick-service foods. The customers of FMC Foodtech fall into two categories:

- Those companies who supply most of the global fast food restaurants that have become household names around the world. Many of the companies that supply food products to your local McDonald's or KFC got their products from FMC Foodtech.

- FMC Foodtech also provides their products to the major wholesalers of processed food, such as Nestle Unilever and Tyson foods.

The global dominance and success of FMC FoodTech is no fluke. They exemplify the concept of *think locally to dominate globally.*

Two of the subsidiary companies at FMC FoodTech are Frigoscandia Equipment and Stein. Frigoscandia Equipment manufactures and develops freezers, chillers and auxiliary equipment designed to preserve the taste, appearance and nutritional value of frozen food. Acquired by FMC in 1996, it is headquartered in Helsingborg, Sweden. Stein, headquartered in Sandusky, Ohio, was founded in 1947 and acquired by Frigoscandia Equipment in 1987. Stein is a world leader in the manufacture of machinery used for the value-added processing of poultry, meat, seafood and vegetables. Stein equipment does everything from cutting, batter and breading, frying, roasting and steaming these types of food products, then Frigoscandia equipment freezes it. Also, in order to test various processing techniques, Stein developed a world-renowned Food Processing Technology Center at its Sandusky headquarters. After being acquired by Frigoscandia, an additional technology center was created in Helsingborg, Sweden. They have assembled some of the brightest talent in the industry to help food processors conduct reliable product and processing evaluations. They also have the analytical tools to help customers test food processing methods and document the findings.

More than 50 percent of the world's frozen food production passes through freezers from Frigoscandia Equipment. Stein owns 75 percent of the U.S. market and is a leading supplier to fast food restaurants globally. So, by all rights, FMC FoodTech could choose to rest on its laurels and demand its customers adjust to their way of business, not the other way around. It doesn't. According to Nicklas Margard, a Swedish national who is regional director Asia Pacific, "Part of our success is that we have locally hired sales and technical staff on the ground in the countries in which we operate. Our direct sales force are experts on the local business environment and culture because they are from that culture. How can I read the body language or subtle language nuances of a customer during a meeting or when negotiating a contract? How am I to know if they are being irrational or stubborn, or if their behavior is normal for that culture? I rely on my local sales force to accurately assess the intentions of our customers."

How do they know what the average consumer in Thailand, Singapore or Malaysia wants in a food product? The answer is a combination of being close to the customer and rigorous research. "We listen to and trust our local sales force in each of these countries," Margard says. They know the consumers' preference in each of their countries better than our staff in Sweden or the United States. Also, representatives from the world's major processed-food suppliers are literally camped out at our Stein Food Processing Technology Center. They test any number of spice and marinade, frying and cooking combinations to match the consumers' regionalized taste requirements." This international focus of FMC FoodTech has become a model of global business success.

For example, one of the fundamental differences Margard learned from his sales team was the consumers' preference, throughout Asia, for dark chicken meat that is processed with the bone intact, whereas in Europe and North America, the customer prefers boneless, white meat chicken products that are lower in fat and considered more healthful. Think about this for a moment: when was the last time you received dark meat chicken nuggets at your local fast food or full service restaurant? In response to this demand, the team at FMC FoodTech developed a unique processing technology and equipment modified to run these new products, that quickly and economically processes the desired "bone-in" wings, thighs and drumsticks. Originally developed for just the local market in Thailand, they now export to countries throughout Asia and their earnings have increased at phenomenal rates for several years running. This process has been repeated with several of the major fast food suppliers and new process lines are continuously being developed in order to meet the local products specifications. "These projects have been driving the growth in the Asia Pacific region, and the process know-how is the most critical for our success," Margard says. "It is not only the individual pieces of equipment that are important; it is the whole process that counts. Foodtech is trying very hard to provide complete solutions to our customers." According to Margard, this specific targeted approach with the unique poultry processing application has been a significant part of FMC FoodTech's growth, accounting for approximately 20 to 25 percent of sales since 1998.

Has FMC FoodTech made mistakes? You bet. Until the mid 1990s, Frigoscandia provided technical field service manuals, written in English, for use by technicians who maintained their commercial freezing units. It's not that Frigoscandia was trying to cut corners by not printing the manuals in a variety of languages, but the result was less than ideal. Part of the periodic maintenance on the freezer required the inside to be washed down with water to rinse residual food particles out. "We found that the technicians were spraying water into the freezer while it was still too cold, even though the technical manual gave specific instructions as to how to conduct the procedure," Margard says. "As a result, we had a $200,000 to $1,000,000 piece of equipment, depending on the capacity of the freezer, that was now completely clogged with ice."

As Margard states, "In analyzing the problem, we realized the disconnect. We had been interfacing directly with the technical managers in our client companies and they all spoke English very well, so we didn't see the need to adapt the manuals. However, once our equipment was installed, the servicing was turned over to local field service technicians, who didn't speak or read English." As a result, Frigoscandia is in the process of localizing all of their field service manuals by writing them in the native languages of the field service technicians.

So, for FMC FoodTech, their local and global success boils down to a few approaches that can benefit any organization.

- Listen to and trust the opinions of the locally hired sales force.
- Willing to redesign equipment or maintenance procedures to meet regional needs.
- Check the ego at the door.

Many technology driven companies suffer from the "not invented here" syndrome and disregard information that could be of use. FMC FoodTech realized that even the best minds of the American food scientists at the Stein Food Processing Technology Center in the United States would not be able to determine the regional tastes of their customers around the world. Such basic concepts as how crispy, flaky, or juicy a breaded piece of chicken should be could not be determined on a per-country basis without first collaborating with food scientists from those countries. So, instead of dismissing the opinions of scientists outside their corporate think tank, they invited scientists and specialists from their customer groups around the world to join them and tackle the problem together.

PEBBLE BEACH COMPANY:
FLEXIBILITY = LONGEVITY

How does a company survive for more than 80 years, including several ownership changes, and still enjoy constant success? The answer is outstanding service to customers and employees alike.

Pebble Beach Company, in Pebble Beach, California, is the parent company of three world-class resorts and four golf courses. The resorts include The Lodge at Pebble Beach, The Inn at Spanish Bay and Casa Palmero. The golf courses include Pebble Beach Golf Links, The Links at Spanish Bay, Spyglass Hill Golf Course and Del Monte Golf Course. Pebble Beach resorts and golf courses are known worldwide for their stunning oceanfront location, peerless quality and outstanding service. Their 1,600 employees display a level of professionalism and proficiency unmatched in the industry. It is a common destination for people from around the world, from avid golfers to those who simply want to enjoy the peaceful environment.

Don't Rest On Your Laurels

Founded in 1919, Pebble Beach Company is home to the AT&T Pebble Beach National Pro-Am Golf Tournament, and has hosted the U.S. Open Golf Championship four times. In spite of this fame and success, Pebble Beach Company doesn't rest on its laurels.

"We have guests who come from all over the world and employees from a variety of backgrounds. As a result, we have a number of guests and employees who speak English as a second language," states Janine Chicourrat, general manager of the Lodge at Pebble Beach, the Beach and Tennis Club, Casa Palmero and the Spa at Pebble Beach. "We want to make sure employees and guests are comfortable in this environment, so we have taken steps to ensure this happens." One of the small details the Pebble Beach Company doesn't overlook is something as simple as a daily greeting. A common compliment from guests at the property is that the employees greet them constantly. So, whether a guest is walking by a gardener or golf pro, the odds are that the guest will be greeted with a warm "good morning" or "good afternoon." The result is a comment stated by many guests: "I don't feel invisible when I am there. They greet me when I am shopping, or just walking to and from my room."

Education Is The Key

Chicourrat and the other members of the management team know that it is up to them to help create an environment where employees and guests can interact so well. To foster this "high touch" approach, the company encourages employees to develop a certain level of competency with the English language. So, the Pebble Beach Company sponsors free English classes in the evenings for their employees. "We hope that the courses will help our multinational employees feel more comfortable using English and greeting our guests," Chicourrat says. Of course, evening classes will only go so far with language proficiency, so the company takes this a step further by providing interpreters for employees when needed. When conducting annual performance reviews for employees who have limited English skills, the company provides professional interpreters to assist the process.

It's All in the Details

An example of where the Pebble Beach Company goes above and beyond the call with international guest services is how it approaches visitors from Japan. The company recognizes the stellar reputation it has in Japan, and enjoys a large number of Japanese guests. As a result, Japanese guests are provided rooms that have room service menus written in Japanese, as well as a special menu that lists Japanese-style meals. Even the smallest details are taken care of. An example is the "no smoking" signs, written in English, that are in all of the guest rooms on the property. Smoking is not allowed in any of the rooms. So, in order to avoid any embarrassing situations, Japanese-language versions, written in perfect, formal Japanese, are placed in rooms where Japanese guests will stay.

Given the number of guests who come from all over the world, the Pebble Beach Company has taken steps to ensure the fewest number of language-based problems arise. An approach the company has taken that is low in cost, yet high in return, is to create a database of those employees who speak languages other than English. The concierge desk has the list, so an employee from anywhere on the property, such as in a golf or other merchandise location, knows that help is just a phone call away.

It would be so easy for an international icon such as the Pebble Beach Company to merely sit back and refuse to adjust its business approach. Yet, through the simple, meaningful touches ranging from company-sponsored language classes, and recognizing and utilizing the unique linguistic abilities of all employees, to bilingual signage, they send a strong message: Guests and employees are equally important.

One sign of success is the number of accolades the company has received in the past, which are numerous. Another sign of success is what they are doing in the present. "Golf Digest" ranked the Pebble Beach Golf Links as the number one golf course in America, in it's 2001-2002 biennial ranking of America's 100 Greatest Golf Courses. This was the first time a public course has been so honored and is another result of the company's continuous drive to improve.

NORTHSTAR-AT-TAHOE: CREATING A MULTINATIONAL TEAM

Survival in the intensely competitive ski and snowsport business involves much more than a great mountain and lots of snow. So, what does it take? As in many industries, one strategy is to merge with other companies, then leverage the benefits of synergy and enhanced purchasing power. Another is to expand one's customer base by attracting an international clientele. Northstar-at-Tahoe has done both and become the premier family snowsport resort in the world-famous Lake Tahoe region that straddles portions of the states of California and Nevada.

Northstar-at-Tahoe is a member of Booth Creek Ski Holdings, Inc., which includes Sierra-at-Tahoe and Big Bear Mountain in California; Waterville Valley, Cranmore Mountain Resort and Loon Mountain in New Hampshire; and the Summit at Snoqualmie in Washington. Booth Creek Ski Holdings is the fourth largest operator of ski resorts in the United States.

After Booth Creek acquired Northstar-at-Tahoe from Fiberboard Corporation in 1996, it implemented a huge program to upgrade and renovate the facilities and the operations.

So, what does this mean for the business? For the second year in a row, "Ski Magazine" has ranked Northstar among the top 60 resorts in North America. The annual readers' poll placed Northstar 22nd overall among North American ski areas, and in the top four of all California resorts. Northstar was also recognized for having the best family programs in California (ranking sixth in North America), and the best grooming operation of all Lake Tahoe Resorts (rated 10th in North America). An upcoming issue of "Child Magazine" also includes Northstar in its list of 10 top family ski resorts.

They have taken all the right steps with the facilities side of the business and their domestic customer base. What about the international clientele and why even pursue that group? Kurt Althof, destination sales manager of Northstar, states, "Of course, we appreciate all guests who come to our resort. However we have found that our international guests stay one week or longer, as compared to our local visitors who stay two days over the weekend."

Adaptations

In an effort to make the mountain and their resort more user-friendly for their international clientele, Northstar-at-Tahoe has made a number of changes in the way they do business.

They have expanded their website to include seven languages, including French, German, Spanish, English, Portuguese, Chinese and Japanese.

They have have added signs and information that describe important information about the resort using the metric system. "What good is a description of the vertical drop of a certain run (a term used by ski resorts to explain the difference in elevation from the top of the run to the bottom of a run) if it is only in feet?" asks Althof. "We provide signage in feet as well as meters and display the temperature in Fahrenheit as well as Celsius."

They have run in-language advertisements in Japanese- and Chinese-language periodicals to attract the large Asian population from throughout California and the west coast.

They have recruited international staff residing abroad and in North America.

"It is very helpful to have the Spanish-speaking employees from Argentina who, in addition to being expert ski instructors, can conduct classes for our Spanish-speaking guests," states Tom Dougherty, employee services supervisor. In fact, Northstar recruits seasonal staff from a variety of countries. Some of these employees are part of a student work exchange program and come to the United States under a 4-month, J-1 visa, through agencies such as Work Experience USA or Council on International Educational Exchange. Many of the students fill positions in the rental shop, in food and beverage or work as lift operators and their bilingual ability is a definite benefit when interacting with the many foreign guests Northstar attracts. The experienced professionals such as ski instructors, ski patrol and snow makers enter under the H2B visa and stay the entire season. Many of the employees on this program come from Argentina, Brazil, Peru, New Zealand, Australia, and Europe.

Recruiting
So, how does Northstar actually attract the international staff? Dougherty and other staff members actually go on recruiting trips to countries in South America and send flyers to

Australian and New Zealand winter resorts. "We found that we don't need to go on these trips every year because once we have attracted employees from these areas, we let word-of-mouth advertising do the recruiting for us," he says. As an example, the Northstar team recruited in Sao Paulo and Rio, Brazil three years ago. The following season, even without taking a trip to South America, they had a fourfold increase in the number of qualified applicants from Brazil.

One of the reasons for this is the emphasis Northstar places on treating employees as well as guests with the utmost respect. In fact, two of the four values of the parent company, Booth Creek Ski Holdings address this: *Booth Creek is committed to our guest's experience. Booth Creek is committed to our employees.*

Easy enough to say or print in company literature, but Northstar breathes life into these values. The following are four examples of how the human resources team goes above and beyond the call to ensure the international employees are cared for.

1) During employment or placement interviews with international candidates, the human resources team is careful to paint a very detailed picture of both the demands of the job the candidate is applying for, as well as a physical description of the location of Northstar-at-Tahoe property. As Dougherty explains, "Not all of our international employees are professional ski instructors, so we are careful to find out if the candidates are comfortable living in a relatively small mountain town with a lot of snow."

2) They assist in finding housing for the students and employ-

ees. If housing in local towns and cities is tight, the staff at Northstar has a unique approach to expanding the market. Much of the housing in the Lake Tahoe area is vacation properties. Many of the homes and condominiums are empty, or rarely used during much of the ski season. In addition, many local homeowners may have extra rooms in their homes and could use extra income to offset the high cost of living in the area. So, to get some relief from the impacted rental market in the Lake Tahoe area, the HR team came up with a creative idea to fill those empty rooms. They came up with an incentive program for the owners, known as "rental rewards" that encourages them to rent those empty rooms during the winter. Incentives come in the form of free ski lift passes to sweeten the pot, in addition to the rental fee charged to the employees. As Dougherty says, "We take great pains to recruit, hire and train a great staff and we don't want them to have a bad experience here. If their experience is bad, it will spread to our guests. So, the housing manager and I spend a lot of time meeting and greeting our international employees at the local, Reno, Nevada, airport and we make sure they have comfortable, convenient housing arrangements. We even provide a morning and evening shuttle service for our employees who live in Reno and the outlying area. This has proven to be so convenient that several of the other local ski resorts have partnered with us to provide the shuttle service for their employees."

3) Welcoming new employees to a company, at the beginning of a busy season, via new-hire orientations is a time-tested method to help ensure consistency of service and content employees, and Northstar does a great job of this. In the fall, at the beginning of every ski season, new-hire training and

the company orientation are conducted in Spanish as well as English. "We realize that not all of our employees are completely comfortable with English, so we want to introduce the company to them in a language they fully understand," states Dougherty. This is followed up by Spanish-language on the job training. This approach is all well and good and more and more companies strive to follow the same model, although not enough offer bilingual orientations and training. But what about at the end of the season, when part-time and seasonal employees are let go? Usually, it is a mad dash for the door, with neither employee nor employer taking much time to do anything but sign paperwork, or make sure keys and uniforms are returned. Not at Northstar, which leads us to point number four.

4) Northstar looks at the end of one season as an opportunity to set the stage for a successful *next* season. According to Dougherty, "We want to find out from our employees, especially our international team, about their experience. Was their experience as an employee what they expected? Was the housing satisfactory? And, most important, were there differences in management styles, compared to their home culture, that were problematic? We want to know about their whole experience, from training to teamwork and we hold employee focus groups at the end of the season to gather this information." Information gained during these sessions has helped the management team at Northstar adjust their approach. They have made many changes, including: adding the in-language orientation programs, translating I-9 tax forms into Spanish, and altering their recruiting and hiring process to ensure prospective employees know precisely what will be expected

of them. Much of this is sound advice even for employers who don't bring on staff from overseas locations.

Benefits

The international approach taken by Northstar-at-Tahoe has resulted in a number of benefits. In addition to having a top-notch local staff, they have a service-oriented and loyal international employee base. This enables them to attend to the needs of local guests as well as guests who come from foreign locations.

"Another benefit of hiring international staff is their knowledge of their home markets and this has helped us in our marketing efforts in these countries," says Althof. "One of the Australian employees working at the resort gave me valuable information about an Australian magazine. A sales representative from the magazine contacted me about purchasing some advertising space in one of their publications, but I didn't know if this particular magazine actually had the readership the sales guy was touting. I asked our Australian employee about the magazine and she confirmed that it was a popular publication and that it did reach the audience and market that the sales man had claimed."

Yet another benefit recognized by Althof came when he was preparing to go on one of the annual "Ski USA" marketing trips he takes to a number of countries to introduce the resort to targeted international customer audiences. Before departing, the same Australian employee encouraged Althof to tone down his sales approach and "to avoid being overbearing," lest he alienate the audience he was trying to encourage visiting Northstar. The process Althof described is precisely what was introduced in chapters two and three. Basically, it is the process of relying upon an internal "culture coach," then leveraging that person's inherent cultural knowledge to assess one's own usual approach, (in Althof's case, too aggressive). Once armed with the new cultural knowledge, it is then up to the person to style-switch into a cultural mode that will be more pleasing to customers in the target culture or cultures. As an example of style switching, Althof goes on to say, "As a result of having meetings with the international staff, I have learned a culturally appropriate approach for getting a new product to market in Brazil. I was coached by our international employees to use Brazilian sales representatives to help spread the word of Northstar-at-Tahoe. In addition, I was cautioned to establish a good personal relationship with the sales representatives before jumping into business discussions. So, I meet with prospective representatives over breakfast, in a casual setting. This personal touch is in direct contrast to the approach I typically use in the United States, where much of my business is conducted over the telephone and I enter into contracts with marketing representatives I've not even met." Indeed, what would be considered by many as a waste of time in the United States is a business necessity in many cultures: establish a personal relationship first, then conduct business.

The Bottom Line

In addition to all of the benefits already mentioned, how has Northstar done from a financial standpoint? Well, according to Althof, the resort has grown fourfold in the last two years, with the vast majority of growth potential yet to come. "The international program is relatively new and it takes time to develop international markets," he says. Without getting into precise dollar amounts, Althof does provide some compelling data: "It is difficult to say exactly how much more they (the international guests) spend but the average stay is eight nights for the international markets and only 2.8 nights for the local, drive market. We know that spending is higher for those guests who choose to stay in our accommodations than those for those who visit the resort for the day.

"Another fact to consider is that the international traveler is quite wealthy, keeping in mind it is quite expensive to visit the U.S. This is due to the negative exchange rate against the dollar that many countries have, excluding the U.K. Hence, the average international visitor is in a higher income bracket than most domestic visitors."

Certainly, Northstar enjoyed visits from international guests even before it embarked on its program of internationalization. But it is all too coincidental that they happen to be enjoying a fourfold increase in international visitations *since* they began the strategy *and* in spite of exchange rates that should, by all accounts, discourage international visitors. As every other company highlighted in this chapter, Northstar-at-Tahoe is not about to rest on its laurels. It is just beginning an ambitious redevelopment of the entire resort that will, as Althof claims, "make our product an even better fit for the international visitor."

STARBUCKS: CREATING A SENSE OF COMMUNITY

With nearly 900 coffeehouses in 22 markets outside North America and, as stated in company literature, "Our passion transcends language and culture," it would be easy to presume this case study is about the international success of Starbucks. It is not. It would be easy to jump to the conclusion that this case examines the Starbucks approach to dealing effectively with foreign customers in the North American market. It is not.

This case highlights a Starbucks store that has done an unparalleled job of style switching, using culture coaches, and demonstrating incredible sensitivity to the needs of a linguistic minority group. It has done this simply by following these key principles that are part of their mission:

- Giving back to the communities in which they are located.

- Building community.

- Embracing diversity as an essential component in the way they do business.

- Develop enthusiastically satisfied customers all of the time.

With historical roots dating back to 1971, Starbucks opened its first location in Seattle's Pike Place Market; it was then known as Starbucks Coffee, Tea and Spices. However, the Starbucks that is so well known today had its beginnings in 1987, when Howard Schultz, a former Starbucks director of retail operations and marketing and some local investors, acquired Starbucks assets and changed its name to Starbucks Coffee Company. Since then, the Starbucks name has become synonymous with creativity, growth, success, and, of course, great service. We all know the basic product is by no means new or unique. The technology required for processing the basic product has been around forever and is not proprietary.

So how has Starbucks transformed coffee, the king of commodity products, into their own private franchise domestically and internationally? Simple. They practice what they preach. The four principles listed above are only a small sampling of the values that help set Starbucks apart. Their mission statement sets the stage for those principles:

"Establish Starbucks as the premier purveyor of the finest coffee in the world while maintaining our uncompromising principles while we grow."

It doesn't end with this. Starbucks also has a separate mission statement dedicated to the environment:

"Starbucks is committed to a role of environmental leadership in all facets of our business."

Building Something From Nothing

Through their combination of principles and values, Starbucks Coffee Company has created coffeehouses that serve more than beverages to their customers; they serve an experience and a sense of community. They attract employees, called partners, who do more than make and serve those beverages; they help create the experience and sense of community. Kelli Caires, one of the thousands of store managers in the Starbucks organization, sets an example that is one we can all strive to attain. Her approach to creating a great customer experience and a sense of community exemplifies the cultural sensitivity that is so greatly needed, and appreciated, in this day and age of constant change and indifference.

Caires is the store manager of a Starbucks located in

Orange County, California.

The store is located in a shopping mall called The Block, one of the newer, "outdoor entertainment" malls that combines indoor and outdoor shopping experiences for their customers. Caires has been the store manager for most of the four years it has been open. On the busiest days of the week, Fridays, Saturdays and Sundays, it is not uncommon for the store to average 1,500 customer visits, with most of those visits in the evening.

This case really begins when Caires and one of her staff, a partner named John, noticed a group of about 40, hearing-impaired, customers visiting the store on a regular basis. "At first, we didn't notice the pattern, but we realized a fairly large group of about 40 customers was coming monthly, on Friday evenings," says Caires. "I knew that John was able to use sign language, because he had children who were hearing impaired, so I asked him to approach the group and find out more about them."

John found out that they were part of an organized social group and that they met at Starbucks every second Friday of the month to visit. With John's assistance as an interpreter, Caires welcomed the group and encouraged them to continue using the store as a gathering place. Then, in her effort to create a unique experience and sense of community for the group, Caires put into motion a series of steps reflecting a cultural and linguistic sensitivity is rarely found in multinational organizations, much less neighborhood stores. In addition to making sure John was scheduled on the evenings they arrived, she made a number of accommodations for her customers. "I didn't want the hearing-impaired customers to feel like they had to use the register where John was working because it might make them feel uncomfortable being singled out," she says. "Also, I didn't have any other employees who could sign, so we had to come up with creative ways to communicate to handle the group." So, she and her team of partners implemented the following strategies:

As a first step, she provided a pad of paper and a pen for every non-signing partner. This enabled them, via writing, to communicate with the hearing-impaired customers. Then, one of the partners came up with a great strategy to speed up the ordering process. He transferred the menu that was posted on the wall behind the counter, onto sheets of paper creating smaller menus. He then laminated these new menus and put one at each register with erasable marking pens. Customers could then simply circle their order on the menu, making the whole process much easier for customer and partners alike. "This was a whole lot easier than expecting these customers to clarify what they wanted to order by pointing to the large menu way up on the wall," says Caires.

To further refine their process, Caires and her team decided to alter one of their long-standing operating procedures. Typically, when customers order a coffee or mixed beverage at Starbucks, the order taker writes the customer's name and specific drink, in black ink, on the cup itself. Then, when the order is ready, another partner calls out the customer's name to let them know the order is ready for pick-up at the counter. In the case of the hearing-impaired customers, Caires' team decided to use a red pen to write the customer's name and order on the cup. The red ink served as a prompt to other Starbucks partners who call out the prepared orders. "I can't think of anything worse than standing there calling out the name of a customer who is hearing-impaired," says

Caires. Indeed, that would be rude to the hearing-impaired customer and a potential source of frustration to the hearing customers. So, when one of the drinks with red ink was ready, John would be summoned to step up and use sign language to call the customers to the counter.

Even with these arrangements in place, Caires wanted to take one more step. As she says, "I was getting frustrated, as were some of the partners, by our inability to communicate directly with our customers. I decided to learn some basic sign language." Then, in a stroke of incredible good timing and luck, a person who represented a subsidiary of Goodwill Industries approached Caires. He offered to have one of his staff members teach sign language to Caires and her staff, free of charge. Caires accepted, then worked out an even better scenario. She invited customers to attend as well. "I thought that some of the hearing customers, who came on those Fridays when our hearing-impaired customers gathered, might want to learn sign language as well. So, I designated Tuesday evenings as lesson nights." All Starbucks partners knew participation was strictly voluntary. Also, as a practical businessperson, Caires made the store available as a classroom on Tuesday evenings because those were the slowest evenings of the week. "At first, I was worried that no one would show up for the lessons, that I might be the only student," she says. Well, on this rare occasion, she was dead wrong. On the first evening the classes were offered, 35 people showed up for lessons. Five were Starbucks partners and 30 were customers! "The lobby of the store was overflowing with people attending the lesson and, when other people walking through the mall saw the activity, many came in to see what was going on," Caires says. So, what was once the slowest night of the week turned into a beehive of activity. Realizing the challenge of teaching essentially a whole new language, the teacher focused on how to sign greetings, salutations, apologies and key phrases used at Starbucks, such as: "Hot?," "Cold?" and "Blended." "As a result of the classes, our hearing-impaired customers truly appreciated our efforts, our partners were more comfortable serving them, and the hearing customers interacted more with the hearing-impaired customers," says Caires. They continued the classes for a full year. Now, those who attended the classes also show up on the Fridays when everyone else gathers.

The Incredible Benefits Of Being Other-Centered

The result? In less than four months, what was once a group of 40 hearing-impaired customers has grown to an *event* that attracts between 300 and 600 hearing-impaired customers each month! And, as Caires' district manager, Kimberly Shelton, states, "Visiting Kelli's store on those Fridays is an amazing sight. There is a virtual sea of people, yet it is relatively silent…everyone is signing." So, in place of the buzz of conversation, there is a tremendous movement of hands; satisfied customers having a great time. To add an even more creative twist, one of partners of the store brought in some of his friends, who participate in a drumming circle, to play music on their drums. "The hearing-impaired customers can't hear the music, but they can feel the beat, so we have a party atmosphere with people dancing and having a great time," says Caires.

Shelton goes on to say, "We actually experienced a slight drop off in business those Friday evenings because other potential customers walking through the mall would see the large crowd and mistakenly presume they would have to wait forever to get served. We can easily handle 1,500 customers on weekend evenings, but other customers didn't realize this. And, quite frankly, we feel so strongly about providing a place of community for our customers that the downturn that one night per month is well worth it." To make life easier for the hearing customers on that one Friday of the month, Caires and her team took extra steps to make sure the access lanes to the counter were kept clear.

The Internet and word-of-mouth advertising has helped spread the Starbucks story throughout the area. Community colleges that offer sign language classes have even called the store to confirm the story, then encourage their students to join the group for "real time" practice sessions. Caires now gets many unsolicited requests for employment from people who can use sign language and want to work at the store. Of a 38-person staff, there are now four partners who can sign fluently. Of course, the other partners know basic salutations and still use the unique "red pen" and laminated menu systems to accommodate the customers.

The business benefits speak for themselves. Under Caires' leadership, the Starbucks at The Block is an unparalleled success. By every measurement Starbucks uses to assess the growth of a store, the Starbucks at The Block far surpasses other stores opened at the same time. Aside from the business benefits, Caires shares two examples that make all of the effort well worth it: "We had a had an older, hearing-impaired, couple from Sweden extend their vacation to the United States by one week just so they would be in town that second Friday of the month. We were able to provide them some comfort in a foreign country by providing a language-friendly environment.

There are also hearing couples that bring in their children just to expose them to a different experience. One of my customers has a two-year-old daughter who could say her name in sign language before she could spell it."

A big part of why Caires works for Starbucks can be summed up in her own words: "At other companies, I might have been slapped on the hand for doing something like this, or wrapped up in bureaucratic red tape. This gives me a chance to be creative and help others."

Indeed. For virtually no cost, Caires and her team of partners have created an environment that is a fine example of combining great customer service with cultural sensitivity.

FROM 'LOCAL SERVICE" TO "GLOBAL SERVICE:" THE LESSON

The cases presented in this chapter illustrate a range of approaches that can be taken to ensure the needs of the multicultural/minority customer or employee base is being attended to. The examples range from: the simple, low-cost and easily implemented, such as the case of what Starbuck's did with its hearing impaired customers, to the complex model detailed in Continental Airlines' Latinization and Capture The Power Of Diversity programs. The examples and lessons from these world leaders present a compelling argument that cannot be ignored: customers and employees want both products and services that meet their unique cultural, linguistic and physical needs. Hence, the hallmark of any successful organization in the coming decades will be the ability to be flexible and adapt to the multiple demands of an ever-changing labor force and customer base. Organizations that accept and act upon this reality will be in the position to reap the benefits of a stable workforce and expanded, loyal customer base.

CHAPTER FIVE

EXCUSE ME, WHAT DID YOU SAY?

CROSS-CULTURAL COMMUNICATION: THE KEYS TO BECOMING "MULTI-LINGUAL" EVEN IF YOU'RE NOT

Working with customers and employees from cultures other than your own can be a challenge if you and they don't share a common language. And the odds of you being fluent in the many languages of all of your non-native customers and employees is pretty slim. In addition, even if you had the desire and the time, learning a second or third language, as an adult, is a daunting task. This doesn't mean, however, that you can't take steps to dramatically improve your ability to communicate with those from other cultures. Let's look at two vitally important components to consider to ensure effective cross-cultural communication:

#1 Understanding "Communication Style"
#2 Using "Culture Friendly" English

COMPONENT #1
UNDERSTANDING "COMMUNICATION STYLE"

So, what are the keys to effectively communicating across the cultural and linguistic gaps that have the potential to come between you and your multinational customers and co-workers? The first step is to remember the iceberg model introduced in chapter two and one of the key messages it held. Specifically, the concept that the common sense held by one group of people or culture is not necessarily shared by another culture. Our beliefs, values and "common sense" are typically under the waterline of the iceberg and, since these are not as obvious as a clothing style or skin color, for example, they are not usually recognized nor understood by those from other cultures.

One of the things our common sense influences is *how* we communicate, whether it be our written language, spoken language or our body language. It is important to note that of the many items listed as residing above the waterline on the iceberg, our body language and spoken language and tone of voice are some of the most impactful. We form initial opinions about the people we meet, and they about us, based upon a variety of factors, but our spoken words and body language play huge roles in influencing those opinions. The role of culture on the way we communicate can be summed up as our *communication style.*

Although there is a great deal of variety in the way people

communicate, cultures influence people's styles of communication. This is because the values and communication styles of cultures tend to act as filters; these filters help those who are communicating to determine if the messages being sent and received are appropriate or inappropriate to the situation. There are numerous examples of people from different cultures using English as a common, international language of business, who have tremendous communication problems due to the *style* each culture used when communicating. Certainly, individuals within a given culture can behave and communicate in unique ways; individual personalities dictate this. However, the common sense of a culture also serves to put boundaries around what is considered appropriate versus inappropriate communication practices, whether they be verbal or non-verbal. The ability to communicate enables people to interact when carrying out any number of activities. The list of communication activities is virtually endless, so for the purpose of highlighting some of the topics in this book let's take a look at just a few:

- Negotiating A Price
- Greeting Customers
- Offering Praise
- Accepting Praise
- Indicating Agreement
- Indicating Disagreement
- Offering Criticism
- Accepting Criticism
- Leading A Meeting
- Participating In A Meeting

Of course, depending upon the values of a culture, these activities can be communicated in different ways. In addition to verbal communication, there are a number of non-verbal tools available that could be used as part of the communication process, including:

- Hand Gestures
- Body Posture
- Personal Space
- Use Of Silence
- Touching
- Eye Contact
- Facial Expressions

Since culture affects communication style, accurate communication is not guaranteed just because two people speak the same language; using the same words does not guarantee success. This was made painfully clear in the case of the cleaning of the haunted mansion at Tokyo Disneyland outlined in chapter three. In addition, there are instances where the words themselves are not the problem, but it is the order in which they appear: some cultures value a more indirect approach, while others appreciate a more indirect style.

Direct Versus Indirect Approaches[i]
The diagrams on the next page illustrate dramatically different approaches to communicating a message, direct versus indirect. Of all the communication style differences, these two alone can be the root of much cross-cultural misunderstanding. In this case, imagine it is a telephone call

(however, these diagrams could easily represent a face-to-face dialogue or a written message.) Diagram A illustrates a typical, direct, approach used in North America, particularly in the United States. Diagram B illustrates a more indirect approach, not uncommon to many countries around the world. Let's call diagram A the diamond style and diagram B the hourglass style. The diamond represents the style often used by people from cultures that value a more direct communication style. "Mean what you say, say what you mean" and "Don't make me read your mind, tell me what's going on" are phrases representative of a culture that values the spoken word, explicitly spells out what is needed and leaves little to conjecture. Edward Hall, a well-known anthropologist best known for his work in intercultural communication, identifies this direct style of communication as the preferred style of people from a "low context" culture. The hourglass represents the style often used by people from cultures that value indirectness, don't need words to communicate a thought when non-verbals or the situation alone may suffice. Hall calls this a "high context" culture, where the context, or situation can carry more weight than words.

"A" THE DIAMOND

"B" THE HOURGLASS

THE BOTTOM LINE
"What's the status
of our order?"

WARM-UP
"Thank you for your
continued support.
We appreciate your help"

"How is your
business volume?"

SUPPORTING DATA
"One of our biggest
accounts is screaming
for this. We need you
to deliver it on time or
we'll find someone
who can"

THE BOTTOM LINE
"We have a very important
customer we need to
support with your product.
I would like to confirm the
delivery date."

CLOSE
"So we can expect it
by Friday? Thanks."

CLOSE
"Thank you for your
help. Sorry to have
caused you any
trouble."

The Diamond

Starting with the diamond, notice the similarity of the message found at the pointed top, the wide middle and pointed bottom zones. These three zones represent, from top to bottom, the beginning, body and end of a verbal or written message. The pointed areas at the beginning and end of the interaction represent the relative lack of time spent in these zones. This approach is widely taught in schools, public speaking courses and business writing classes. Although it doesn't have a formal name, I like to call it the *Three T Approach*, with each T representing one of the three zones.

The first T

Tell them what you *will* tell them. It is a precursor to the main body, a teaser of what is to come, the "bottom line." In written form, this is the first, or introductory sentence of the paragraph.

The second T

Tell them. This is an embellishment of the first T and contains the main body of data or information that builds upon the first T. In written form, this is the body of the paragraph.

The third T

Tell them what you *told* them. This is in the past tense and is an overview, a review of what was already said. In written form, this is the closing sentence of the paragraph.

The Three T Approach is a style that is a perfect fit for a culture that tolerates little or no ambiguity and puts task over relationship, especially in business situations. Of course, relationships are valued in the United States, yet the relationship-related words usually come *after* the task has been taken care of. It is unusual to receive a business call from someone, even someone you know, that begins with a lot of time devoted to relationship-oriented words. Most business people start to get antsy after just a few moments and want to get to the bottom line. Consider the following approach and how it could work against the caller, Keith, who is calling his business associate, Allison:

Scenario #1:

Keith: *"Hi Allison, this is Keith, how are you today?"*

Allison: *"I'm fine, how are you?"*

Keith: *"Just great, thanks. I was wondering how your golf game went last weekend."*

Allison: *"Oh, it was fine."*

Keith: *"Was the weather good?"*

Allison: *"A little cloudy, but no rain."*

Keith: *"Did you enjoy the day?"*

Allison: (a full 30 seconds has passed at this point and still no reference to the reason Keith is calling, so she needs to take control) *"Yes, all went well, so what's on your mind today?"*

Since the timing of when to use relationship-oriented words is important, let's take a look at another situation between two people from the United States. Consider how the caller, Keith, could alter his approach to be more effective and still take care of relationships in a culturally effective manner. He is now calling another colleague, Amanda:

Scenario #2:

Keith: *"Hi Amanda, this is Keith, how are you today?"*

Amanda: *"I'm fine, how are you?"*

Keith: *"Just great, thanks. Hey, the reason I'm calling is to discuss the XYZ proposal. Do you have a minute now or can we set a time for later in the day?"*

Amanda: *"I'm getting ready for a meeting. Can we set something up for this afternoon, say 1:00 p.m.?"*

Keith: *"Sounds good. I know you have to go, but was your class reunion a success this weekend?"*

Amanda: *"We had a wonderful time, thanks."*

Keith: *"Great, I'll call at 1:00."*

Amanda: *"Thanks, talk to you then."*

In this second case, the caller limits his salutations to a generic "how are you," then jumps right into the reason for his call. And once the business has been taken care of, the two engage in a brief exchange that reflects their friendship. Finally, the confirming statement, "I'll call at 1:00" closes the call.

The Hourglass

The second diagram, the hourglass, represents a communication style that is just about the opposite of what was shown in the diamond. Notice the similarity of messages found in the wide top and bottom zones. These wide areas at the beginning and end of the communication represent the relatively large amount of time spent in these relationship-building and maintenance zones during interaction. The narrow zone in the middle represents the portion of the interaction where the speaker "gets to the point." However, you'll notice by the words in the diagram that the words used are a far cry from the bottom line orientation of the words used in the second zone of the diamond. Don't misunderstand the hourglass approach as one that is wishy-washy and easily taken advantage of. A concern for relationships and a tendency to be indirect does not mean business goals will always take back seat to interpersonal goals. Being indirect and less accusatory, verbally, just means those thoughts haven't been spoken.

The point of this chapter is not to say that one style is better than another. Both are quite effective when those in communication have similar cultural backgrounds. The point is to emphasize the communication problems that arise between people from different cultural backgrounds who use different communication styles. The first scenario, in which Keith contacted Allison, was an example of the problems that can arise when those in communication have vastly differing approaches *even though language comprehension wasn't a barrier.* Therefore, it is incumbent upon the service provider to find out the preferred communication style of his customers, then style switch and adopt an approach that will not alienate or upset them. In similar fashion, the department supervisor has the challenge of determining how best to approach her subordinates, then pick and choose from a variety of approaches. Intercultural leadership skills will be explored in more detail in the next chapter.

THE ROLE OF BODY LANGUAGE
AND PERSONAL COMFORT

Choosing culturally appropriate non-verbals can be as important as choosing correct words, or choosing to be direct versus indirect. Consider the importance of body language in the following situation: A person who is comfortable with touching, who stands close to those with whom he is speaking and who maintains direct eye contact is likely to create undue stress in the person who comes from a culture that values more interpersonal space, less or no touching and indirect eye contact.

In fact, as a result of his research on spatial behavior and non-verbal communication, Hall[ii] concluded that North Americans are comfortable standing from about 21 inches to as much as four or five feet from each other when engaged in a discussion. As the topic of the discussion becomes more impersonal, even more distance can be appropriate. Compare and contrast this to Hall's finding that Latin Americans and Arabs prefer about 12 inches of separation if the discussion is at all personal. Can you imagine the pressure that would build up between a Latin American and a North American who are engaged in a conversation? The Latin American could wind up virtually chasing the North American around a room as one advances and the other retreats!

How Voice Tone Sets The Tone

Similarly important is the tone of voice. Voice tone by itself is a powerful communication medium that can be the source of tremendous frustration in cross-cultural situations. It is not uncommon in North America, for example, for misunderstandings to arise between local employees and their customers who are natives of China, Taiwan, Hong Kong, India and Pakistan. Why? Simply the way many people from these cultures use English. To the ear of the North American employee, it can sound like a customer from one of these cultures is overly pushy, rude or upset when, in fact, that isn't the case at all. Some of the following *communication* style issues can lead to native speaker confusion and misinterpretation of the intention of the non-native English speaker:

- Misplaced stress on certain words, harsh tone of voice, or short vowels.
- Loud voice.
- Lack of softening expressions, such as: "I would like help with … ", "Could you please … ", "I'm afraid that …"

Compare the following two statements and determine which you would rather hear. The situation: A non native-English speaking customer wants to open an account at a bank. He approaches the bank teller and says:

Approach #1: *"I **want** to open an account **today**!"*
Approach #2: *"I would like to open an account today."*

The bolded words in approach #1 indicate where the customer placed stress, hence, raising his voice. To the native speaker of English, this could sound curt or demanding, even though the customer had no intention of sending that message.

Items A and B listed above here have nothing to do with vocabulary and can be some of the most challenging for the non-native speaker to remedy. Even the most proficient non native-English speakers can have tremendous difficulty changing where they place stress in a statement. The third item, C, softening expressions, is one that can take years for the non-native speaker to develop and represents an advanced vocabulary and ability to effectively *interact* in English. This is much more difficult than merely understanding a written document or the words of a native speaker of English.

"CULTURE COACH" TO THE RESCUE:

The situation listed above is not an isolated incident. Unfortunately, there are numerous examples of companies that have fail to prepare their employees to effectively communicate with customers from other countries and, as a result, lose employees. The reason? Employees get tired of dealing with angry or demanding customers. The remedy is relatively simple, yet seldom used. Employees need to understand the communication styles of the foreign national customers they will likely come into contact with. Even if employees never learn the native languages of their multinational customers, they should be made aware of *how* those customers are likely to approach them and then determine appropriate responses. There is one very effective strategy that will help in this area, and it can be accomplished in two ways. The strategy involves using people who know the target culture, culture coaches, a concept explained in chapter three. One source of culture coaches can be from within the company. These likely candidates are employees who are either from the target culture(s) or who have a deep knowledge of both the culture and its language. Another source of culture coaches can be from the local community. With the increasing numbers of immigrants, more adult education classes are being offered to help them learn English. Why not employ either some of the adult students in these classes, or those who are teaching the classes, to be culture coaches? Let's take a look at how culture coaches can be used to assess the effectiveness of the communication style used in an organization.

CULTURAL EFFECTIVENESS ON-THE-JOB ASSESSING YOUR COMMUNICATION STYLE: YOUR WORDS, TONE, AND ACTIONS

A fundamental of cross-cultural effectiveness is the willingness and ability to constantly assess the impact of one's approach on a target culture or cultures. This assessment tool can be used as a way to gather real-time data about the effectiveness of your cross-cultural customer service. It is also useful as a training exercise. This is designed to get you to think more purposefully about your language, demeanor, and the general impression you give customers from other countries. From your customers' perspective, do you show interest, sincerity and respect with the words you use, your tone of voice, and your everyday actions? Many non-native customers are especially sensitive to signs of disrespect because, as members of a minority group, it is possible their needs are often overlooked by service providers. So you need to be especially sensitive to how you treat them to avoid offending them. This assessment will help you zero in on those behaviors and communication styles that are either especially offensive to your customers from different cultures or culturally appropriate. The goal is to recognize and maximize your strengths and recognize and then minimize your areas of weakness.

The key to success is to involve your culture coaches in the process. For each question, it is important to expose your culture coaches to a realistic setting and scenario; they need to see what actually happens on the job, whether face-to-face, via the Internet, or over the telephone. For example, in the case of a retail store, actually have the culture coaches walk into the store and assess business interactions as a "secret shopper." Secret shoppers have been used for years; this simply adds the cultural aspect to that approach. If it is not possible to use an actual work environment, it is quite easy to recreate a scenario elsewhere. Simply have two native speakers of English role-play a customer/employee situation, then have your culture coaches observe and analyze the interaction. The key is to make it as realistic as possible.

Have your culture coaches observe an interaction, either as a secret shopper or after observing employees role-play a typical scenario. For each observation or question, ask your culture coaches to assess the approach using the checklist below. If you are using an appropriate approach, have your culture coach specify exactly what is working so you can duplicate the success. On the other hand, if your culture coach identifies less than appropriate interactions, get specific feedback about what was not working, then suggestions for improvement. Regardless of your approach, the goal is to increase the cultural sensitivity of the team. With a heightened sensitivity, a team can then determine future strategies to ensure product lines, store layouts, web designs and sales techniques are culturally appropriate. The following questions are just a sampling of what you can use. Determine you own set of questions and areas to assess based upon the needs of your business and customers.

Communication Style In Action: How Do You Rate?

Your Tone/Pace
1) Do you sound busy or are you easily interrupted? If you do, how can you become more approachable and enthusiastic?
2) Are you responsive to the customer's mood? If not, what

can you do to become more responsive?

3) Is your pace too fast or direct? If so, how can you slow down and be more indirect?

4) Are you speaking clearly and loud enough? If not, what can you do to speak more clearly and loudly? Or how you can become more sensitive to know if you are speaking clearly and loudly enough?

Your Words

1) Do your words match your tone of voice? If not, what can you do to match your tone of voice to your words?

2) Are you using internal jargon that the customer doesn't understand? If so, how can you avoid doing this? What should you say instead?

3) Are you using the customer's name? Is that appropriate? If not, how can you best address the customer?

4) Are your explanations of the product easy to understand? If not, how can you best explain the product?

Your Actions

1) Are you slouching or leaning against something, when you shouldn't be? If so, how can you stop doing this? What is appropriate posture?

2) Are you eating, chewing gum, smoking, or having personal conversations with co-workers instead of interacting with customers? What do your customers expect?

3) Do you have direct eye contact with your customer? Is eye contact appropriate? What can you do to improve your eye contact?

4) How appropriate is your non-verbal behavior? Facial expressions, hand movement, proximity to the customer?

How can you improve your non-verbals?

COMPONENT #2
USING "CULTURE-FRIENDLY" ENGLISH

Communicating In English Across Cultures

Non-native speakers of English, or those who speak very little English, have at least two major communication challenges in North America and in particular, the United States. First of all, relative to other countries in the world, the number of native-born bilingual Americans is embarrassingly low. According to William P. Rivers, associate of language policy at the National Foreign Language Center at the University of Maryland, of the 14 to 16 million college students in the United States alone, only about 8 percent study a foreign language, or about 1.2 million students. Of those, only half will continue their studies beyond the second year of college, leaving about 600,000 students. Then, of these 600,000, only 10 percent will attain a level of working proficiency in the language. To compound the situation, many don't use their linguistic skills after leaving college so they forget them.

Second, many Americans compound their linguistic deficiencies by making their English harder to understand for the non-native speaker. While not done as an intentional effort to confuse, the communication style of many Americans does just that. Word choice, speed of interaction and misguided attempts to simplify grammatical structure are the culprits in many cases.

Let's take a look at a couple of situations that represent challenges non native-English speakers have to deal with on a regular basis in North America. These, unfortunately, represent approaches used by many Americans who come into contact with non native-speakers of English, both in United States as well as abroad.

Situation #1: "Jeet Yet?"

Several years ago, I attended a conference in the United States with a colleague from Sweden. My colleague, Leif, is multilingual and his English is impeccable. Unfortunately, he has a fairly thick Swedish accent and doesn't speak at the faster-than-light-speed of many Americans, hence he can sound like he has a less than firm command of the language. He and I were seated at a table with six other conference attendees, all of whom were from the United States. As it got close to the lunch hour, one of the attendees turned to Leif and attempted to engage him in a conversation. This is how it went:

Conference Attendee: "Jya wanna join us fer some chow?"

Leif: "Pardon me?" (Said with a perplexed look on his face and in his heavily-accented English)

Conference Attendee: "Jeet yet?" (Rephrasing the statement in an attempt to make it easier to understand)

Leif: "What is it you want to do?" (Now his face shows complete confusion)

Conference Attendee: "You, me, friend (pointing to me), go restaurant, eat food, (This is accompanied by an exaggerated use of the hands to indicate movement of eating utensils to mouth) come back conference." (This was all done in a voice tone that was just a couple of decibels shy of yelling).

Leif: "No, thank you for the invitation, though." (Completely disgusted by the approach the gentleman used).

After turning down the conference attendee, we lunch by ourselves and, in a tone of complete bewilderment, Leif said to me: "Where do you Americans learn how to do that? It sounds like the old Tarzan movies when Tarzan would talk to the chimpanzee, and I cannot tell you how many times I have had people in this country try to communicate with me using that terrible grammar, incomplete sentences and raising their voices." He continued his tirade, in a half-joking mode by asking, "Is it mandatory for all of you to attend some course in high school or university to learn that terribly inappropriate approach for communicating with non-native English speakers?" We both had a good laugh, but the message is clear: There has to be a better way to communicate with non-native speakers, even if most Americans are limited to using English.

Needless to say, the man who interacted with Leif at the conference didn't intend to create a situation in which Leif would feel he was being "talked down to." In fact, his intention was absolutely positive and he undoubtedly thought his approach would help facilitate understanding. Unfortunately, the approach backfired .

Situation #2: "Welcome Aboard"

The following statement was made by an American marketing executive who was welcoming a group of newly hired employees to his division. The comments were made as part of a new-hire orientation the employees were attending. Of the 45 employees, 15 were non-native speakers of English whose command of standard business English was good. They had been hired to help create culturally acceptable marketing campaigns for the many customer groups of the company. Can you identify the phrases that could confuse the non-native speaker?

"Welcome aboard. We're glad to have you join our fine team of all-star players. I know you have all been chosen because you're the cream of the crop and have every confidence you'll make the grade. During your career here, you will undoubtedly face many obstacles, but don't let that derail you. We want you to take the bull by the horns and tackle those issues. As for the company, well, we've been around the block more than a few times, so we are well aware of the challenges in the marketplace. However, that doesn't mean we have all the answers; we are always open to suggestions, so don't hesitate to run new ideas up the flagpole. Don't worry that someone will take your head off for saying something that's completely out of left field. Nothing ventured, nothing gained is my personal guiding light and I want you to take risks. Good luck in your careers!"

How difficult would it have been for the Americans to alter their approaches in these two situations? It is surprisingly simple, but it means consciously choosing appropriate words, phrases, tone of voice and sentence structure. Let's take a look at 15 of the most important areas to adjust when communicating with non-native speakers of English. All of the following approaches can be used when interacting verbally. Those numbers with the asterisk* next to them indicate skills that can be transferred to written communication.

15 APPROACHES TO HELP BRIDGE THE GAP

1) Slow Down. Allow two to four times the amount of time you would typically expect for a response. In fact, after asking a non-native speaker a question, try counting to 10 before asking another question, or rephrasing your original question.

2) Don't Interrupt. Avoid filling silences too soon. The other person may be translating what you said into their native language. Many non-native speakers complain that communicating with Americans is like participating in a rugby match: "Everyone is after the ball (the right to speak) and if you're not quick or aggressive, you get run over or ignored." The following is just part of a conversation I overheard while waiting for a meeting to start. Note the flow of the highlighted words:

Speaker: "I took one of my kids skiing last weekend, but before we got to the resort, we ran into a snow storm and had to put on **tire chains**, it was ..."

Interrupter #1: "Speaking of **tire chains**, I had the same problem last year, I put them on but they broke. I had no choice but to go to a local service station to get some new chains and they really **ripped me off**, they ..."

Interrupter #2: "Oh, I've got a great story about getting **ripped off**. My wife and I recently went on a **vacation** that was supposed to include everything, well..."

Interrupter #3: "Let me tell you about the **vacation** of a lifetime. Last summer I took the family to a great place for **fishing**. We had the place to our...."

Interrupter #4: "Gosh, I haven't gone **fishing** in a long time, just too busy. I'm not sure I could even find my pole, the garage is such a mess!"

All of a sudden, what started out as a story about a man taking his child skiing has devolved into some guy complaining about his messy garage. Sound familiar? It should, because odds are high that you have participated in a similar conversation flow if you have had a conversation with a group of Americans. There is a strong tendency for one person to finish another person's sentence by linking a word already used, the "conversational ball," with a topic or idea the second person wants to introduce. And, in many cases, this isn't considered rude; it is a widely accepted conversation style. Certainly, the interruptions aren't always this blatant and the situation can change if there is a hierarchical pecking order amongst the participants, but the message should be clear: for the non-native speaker, this type of conversational flow is difficult, if not impossible, to participate in.

In a situation such as this, the original speaker has several tools available to maintain control. He can prevent interrupter #1 from "stealing the ball" with a combination of verbal and non-verbal approaches. For example, he could lift his hand (as if a traffic cop stopping a car) then say, "excuse me, let me finish," or "hold on a second." In addition, he could raise his voice and speak faster (thus overpowering the interrupter) and even look away from the interrupter to focus on the people who are still listening. If, however, the original speaker loses the conversational ball, he must counter with his own well timed interruption, such as: "As I was saying about my ski trip," or, if among friends and sarcasm is acceptable, "Before I was so rudely interrupted ..."

3) One Idea Per Sentence. Use simple sentences and avoid unusual question forms.

> Instead of this: *"I wouldn't recommend anything along the lines of an off-site meeting to discuss this. It would be better to hold it on-site, don't you agree?"*
> Try this: *"I do not think we should have the meeting at a local conference center. I think we can hold the meeting here at our office. What do you think?"*

> Instead of this: *"Why don't you consider enrolling in our Platinum Plan, which would save you about 20 percent per month on your service bill and give you access to our 24-hour call center?"*
> Try This: *"We have a payment plan called the Platinum Plan. Can I explain it to you? This plan has two benefits. The first benefit is you will save 20 percent per month on your service bill. The second benefit is you will be able to use our 24-hour call center."*

4) Use Active Instead Of Passive Verbs.

> Instead of this: *"The promotion has been canceled."*
> Try this: *"The promotion is over"* or *"The promotion is finished."*

> Instead of this: *"It has been decided that we will continue the sale another month."*
> Try this: *"We decided to continue the sale another month"* or *"We will continue the sale another month."*

5) Speak Clearly. Enunciate each word and avoid blending two words.

> Instead of these: *Couldja, wouldja, wanna, gonna, hafta, didja*
> Try these: *Could You, Would You, Want To, Going To, Have To, Did You*

6) Don't Use Slang/Colloquial Or Idiomatic Expressions.
Avoid technical terms and acronyms, unless you know your customer or employee knows what they mean.

> Instead of this: *"Let's break out the floor plans of the new store and make sure we have the POS sites dialed in before this place turns into a three-ring circus full of construction workers."* (Said to a team of employees while conducting a walk-through in a retail store under construction.)
> Try this: *"This morning, we need to confirm the location of the point of sale registers. So, let me show you the floor plans while we walk through the store. It is important to do this before 9:00 a.m. After 9:00 a.m., there will be a lot of construction workers and it will be too busy to do this."*

> Instead of this: *"You're gonna love this new digital camera. It's full of bells and whistles and you can review your pictures in the blink of an eye."* (Said to a customer who is comparing cameras.)
> Try this: *"Let me show you this digital camera. It is a model with many benefits and abilities. One of the benefits is the 'review pictures' function. It is two times faster than the other camera I showed you."*

7) Re-Phrase Sentences. Repeat important ideas using different words to explain the same concept. Here are two examples:

A) *"This new type of fabric is stain resistant, so this blouse will be very easy to clean."*

B) *"My presentation today is about employee healthcare options. I will introduce four health insurance plans."*

8) Use Visual Support. Write your message, draw pictures and graphs, use body language.

If conducting a teleconference for employees, send the agenda to all participants in advance. Distribute a "read ahead" list of important issues or questions you need to discuss to all meeting participants. Some non-native speakers learned to read and write English, but spent very little time on speaking and listening skills. Therefore, get in the habit of sending out post-meeting "agreement lists" to the participants so they can read and review the main points or action plans they verbally agreed to during the meeting. Seeing the points in writing can reinforce support of a concept or highlight areas that need to be discussed further.

If explaining a product to a customer, demonstrate its use instead of merely talking about it. Consider preparing data sheets or specification sheets in a variety of languages.

9) Confirm Understanding. Have the other person repeat their understanding of the material or instructions back to you. Avoid using phrases that can be answered with "yes" or "no."

Instead of this: *"Do you understand?"* (After explaining some policy changes to a department supervisor who is a non-native speaker of English.)

Try this: *"Could you explain to me how these changes in the policy will affect your department?"* (Certainly, once you and your counterparts have worked together for a while, you will begin to know if they truly comprehend what you are saying, so you can alter how you confirm understanding.)

Instead of this: *"Do you have any questions about how to program the DVD player?"* (Said to a customer in a retail store.)

Try this: *"Before you leave with your new DVD, let's take a few minutes to review the programming instructions together. So, what would you do for step number one?"* (In a similar fashion, have the customer lead you through the whole series of steps, having him or her demonstrate.)

10) Avoid Negative Contractions. The final letter, the "t" is hard to hear, especially when these types of words are spoken rapidly. These can also be confusing in the written form.

Instead of this: *Can't, Won't, Couldn't, Haven't, Don't*
Try this: *Cannot, Will Not, Could Not, Have Not, Do Not*

11) Use A Normal Tone Of Voice. Believe it or not, raising one's voice doesn't help non-native speakers instantaneously understand English. Do not raise your voice or shout!

12) Focus Your Questions. Help the speaker zero in on the area they are having trouble with

> Instead of this: *"What's the problem?"*
> Try this: *"Please explain the section of the invoice you do not understand."*

13) Ask For Spelling Or Meaning.

> Instead of this: *"What's your name again?"*
> Try this: *"Could you please spell your name?"* or *"Could you please write your name for me?"*

14) Use Proper Grammar. Avoid using the "baby talk" or the "Tarzan talk" that so infuriated my colleague Leif.

15) Be A Culturally Sensitive Speaker and Listener. All of the previous 14 skill points will be less than effective if the native speaker of English doesn't keep in mind the two-way nature of communication: Sometimes you need to speak and sometimes you need to listen. Mainstream business culture puts a premium on verbal communication. Unfortunately, in the United States, many people put more emphasis on *speaking* than on *listening*. However, in the case of non-native speakers of English, cultural differences and language difficulties can combine to reduce their ability to interact and provide feedback. It is not uncommon to hear native speakers react in the following way about non-native speakers: "Does he really understand me?," "Why doesn't she ask any questions?," "Talking to him is like talking to a wall, there is no expression!" On the flip side, it is not uncommon for non-native speakers to complain in the following way about native speakers of English: "Once he starts talking, he never stops?," "I wish her questions were sincere. She never waits for my answer, so I never join the conversation!," "Why do they always finish my sentences?"

Effective communication is more than sending or receiving messages; it involves the speaker and listener working together to reach understanding. By modifying your spoken and written English, you will be more easily and clearly understood by non-native employees and customers. Simple differences in tone of voice or body language can lead to mutually inaccurate interpretations such as "She's not supportive," "He's unreasonable," or "He's too demanding." Modifying your English means taking steps to improve your ability to both *speak* **and** *listen* in a culturally sensitive manner. The four skill areas listed below are invaluable.

INTERACTIVE SPEAKING AND LISTENING[iii]

Skill Area 1: Interrupting (turn-taking)

Interactive Speaking: Allow opportunity for customer or employee to ask questions, to take turns as the speaker. After you ask the speaker a question, give him or her the space to think about your question and time to respond. Count to five in your mind before saying anything else.

Interactive Listening: Let the customer or employee finish his/her thought before you interrupt. Be patient.

Skill Area 2: Focused Clarification

Interactive Speaking: "Please explain" is too broad. Help the customer or employee focus on how you, the speaker, can improve your approach. "What part can I explain to you?"

Interactive Listening: Avoid broad expressions such as "I don't understand." It is better to say, "I understand this, but will you explain the next thing you said?" Avoid exaggerated gestures of not understanding.

Skill Area 3: Confirming

Interactive Speaking: Summarize what you have said, "Let me review what I've said." Use written messages, drawings or body language as support.

Interactive Listening: Confirm your overall understanding of what the customer or employee has said. "Can I confirm what I think you want me to do?"

Skill Area 4: Communication Feedback

Interactive Speaking: Expect less feedback such as eye contact or "uh huh, I see."

Interactive Listening: Indicate that you are listening attentively. Take notes, nod your head, avoid a constant stare.

"WELCOME ABOARD"—REVISITED

Remember the speech from the marketing executive introduced earlier? It is time to clean it up. Let's take a look at how it could be transformed from the version that was filled with slang, difficult words, passive verb forms, and long sentences into a version that is easier to understand. The most obvious problem areas are highlighted. Note how these are changed in the second version and reflect some of the skills introduced in this component for using "culture-friendly" English.

Instead of this:

*"Welcome **aboard**. We're glad to have you join our fine **team of all-star players**. I know you have all **been chosen** because you're the **cream of the crop** and have every confidence you'll **make the grade**. During your career here, you will **undoubtedly** face many obstacles, but don't let that **derail you**. We want you to **take the bull by the horns** and **tackle** those issues. As for the company, well, we've **been around the block** more than a few times, so we are well aware of the challenges in the marketplace. However, that doesn't mean we have all the answers, we are always **open to suggestions**, so don't hesitate to **run new ideas up the flagpole**. Don't worry that someone will **take your head off** for saying something that's completely **out of left field**. **Nothing ventured, nothing gained** is my personal **guiding light** and I want you to take risks. Good luck in your careers!"*

Try this:

"Welcome to the marketing division of XYZ company . We are glad to have you join our fine group of employees in this division. We chose you because you are the most talented and qualified for the job. During your career here, you will probably face many challenges. Please do not worry about them. We want you to deal with the challenges and overcome them. XYZ company is 40 years old, so we are well aware of the challenges in the marketplace. However, that does not mean we have solved all

of the challenges and problems. We are constantly looking for new ways to improve, and want your help. Please let us know when you have new ideas. We value your suggestions. We value your creativity. There is a phrase that I like very much, it is: 'Nothing ventured, nothing gained.' This means that I want you to be creative and think of new ways to beat the competition. Good luck in your careers!"

NO EXCUSES!

Learning another language can be tremendously satisfying and fun. Those who are bilingual or multilingual can and do enjoy many benefits when it comes to interacting and communicating in a medium that is mutually understood. This doesn't mean, however, that those who haven't and won't become proficient in a second or third language have no hope for enjoying effective intercultural communication. This certainly isn't the case, as the opportunities for communication improvement introduced in this chapter should have made abundantly clear. The excuse of "I'm not good at languages" needn't get in the way. Why throw one's hands into the air in desperation when so many relatively simple strategies for improving intercultural communication exist?

If you have the desire and opportunity to learn about the language or languages of your customers and employee base then you should pursue this goal. Even learning a few greetings or salutations is better than nothing. However, it is imperative to balance the learning of foreign languages with the learning of foreign cultures and communication styles. On the flip side, for those who are already fluent in a foreign language, take the time to revisit that language from a cultural perspective. Become as fluent in the preferred communication style of that culture as you are fluent in the spoken or written language.

REINFORCING THE CONCEPTS: TEAM EXERCISES TO IMPROVE COMMUNICATION STYLE

With your understanding of differences in communication styles, think about how both you and your whole team can work together more effectively to better satisfy the communication needs of your multicultural customers. As with the assessment introduced earlier in the chapter, these exercises are most effective when you involve people who know the culture, values and communication styles. These culture coaches will be able to assess your approach and should be prepared to give specific instructions for improvement.

EXERCISE #1

Clean Up The Jargon For Clear Communication

Please read the following statements. Decide if you think the words or statements are as effective as they could be. Rewrite the statements so they are more effective and avoid negative customer perception or miscommunication. Remember, the tone you use will have a major impact on the way the message is interpreted. Change the scenarios to reflect your business situation, your customer base and your multicultural employee base. Discuss how to respond as a team, then practice.

1) "What I'm trying to say is that I can't do that, the program has expired."

2) "Hang on."

3) "Your account number is?"

4) "Yeah."

5) "What you need to do is follow these instructions, then there should be no problems, OK?" (Later, after giving instructions....) "Is that clear?"

6) "Let's block out some time to strategize new approaches and dial in a new roll-out plan."

EXERCISE #2

"Incident" Resolution Practice

Step A:
As a group, choose a typical, challenging customer service incident or problem. Emphasis is on dealing effectively with non-native speakers of English using skills introduced in the chapter. Outline the situation below. Next, based upon your knowledge of the business and advice from your culture coach, determine a strategy to both deal with the business problem **and** the cultural/linguistic problem. Taking care of both ensures exceptional customer service and a more loyal customer base.

"Incident" Outline:

_____

_____

_____

_____

_____

_____

_____

Step B:

To illustrate your strategy, you will act out this situation in front of your colleagues and culture coaches in role-play format. Please choose who will act out the roles of customer service providers and who will be the customers.

Step C: Debrief "Incident" Resolution Practice

As a group, analyze the role-play. Please use the space below to list key learning points discussed during the debriefing of each role-play.

1) Observer's Notes:
What Worked And Why:
What Needs Improvement And Why:

2) Participant's Notes
How did you style switch?
Do you think it worked? Why?
What could be improved? How?

Before discussing the viewpoints of the observers and participants, make sure both groups have had enough time to assess the role-play and write down their observations. Also, before eliciting feedback from the observers, give those who participated in the role-play the opportunity to analyze their performance first.

[i] Hall, Edward T. *Beyond Culture.* New York: Anchor/Doubleday, 1976.

[ii] Hall, Edward T. *The Silent Language.* New York: Anchor/Doubleday, 1959.
Hall, Edward T. *The Hidden Dimension.* Garden City, NY, Doubleday, 1966.

[iii] Adapted From: "English for Intercultural Communication" Intercultural Relations Institute, 1985.

CHAPTER SIX

INTERNATIONAL LEADERSHIP AT HOME: THINK GLOBALLY, ACT LOCALLY

It is quite simple: outstanding, consistent, forward-thinking, creative, never saying "We've achieved market dominance, so now it's time to relax" leadership leads to customer service that eats the competition alive. It's a natural flow. Those who relentlessly pursue and attain leadership excellence also attain second-to-none customer service. Why? Because outstanding leaders are those rare individuals who are able to address the needs of the business, the teams they manage and the customers they serve. Good leaders use any number of approaches to take care of their teams, to provide excellent internal customer service: they choose the correct people for the job; they train those people; they listen to their employees; they let employees know their contributions are appreciated; they hold themselves and others accountable; they make the tough calls; and realize that they are not running for political office. Good leaders and managers know they aren't in a popularity contest, yet they can be immensely popular. The contrary is also quite true: inconsistent, stuck-in-the-rut, quick to take credit, rest on one's laurels and blame-others leadership leads to abysmal customer service. Why? Because the internal health of any organization is the determining factor for the service it provides externally. Treat your internal customers well and they will, in turn, treat your external customers well.

So, you might be asking yourself, "What's new?" There are hundreds of books on this subject. Here' the challenge: Are you equally adept at leading and managing people from your own culture, as well as those who come from different cultural backgrounds? Or, if not yet adept, are you willing to learn different leadership and management approaches that take into account cultural awareness and sensitivity? A major step in this direction, as described in chapter two, is to find out if your positive *intentions* as a leader are being *perceived* as positive by your subordinates. If there is a gap between your intentions and their perceptions, how big is it and what is the most effective way to bridge it?

The companies highlighted in chapter four are full of leaders who both recognize the need to style switch when managing across cultures, then do something about it. As a result, they have reaped amazing benefits both domestically and internationally. The example of Northstar-at-Tahoe exemplifies this concept. They recruit employees from several countries and treat them well. In turn, those employees turn into walking, talking emissaries of good will for Northstar when they return to their respective countries at the end of each season. With the positive recommendations from their international employees, Northstar enjoys a constantly growing base of loyal employees and customers from those countries.

So, what if you are a leader in a much smaller organization, one that has operations based only in United States or Canada and no international offices? Does it mean the examples and approaches highlighted via these successful companies should be discounted as applicable for just the big guys? Absolutely not. The fundamentals of leading and managing effectively across cultures don't change, regardless of organizational size, product line, for-profit or not-for-profit status. By creating a satisfied, self-motivated, creative and loyal team of multicultural employees, you will be much better positioned to attract and retain the ever-expanding number of foreign-born customers.

INTENTION VERSUS PECEPTION: WHO IS RIGHT?

We have already dispelled the myth that when people are interacting, the positive intentions of those who are sending the messages are always perceived as positive by those receiving the messages. This is a challenge even when the two participants are from similar backgrounds, and particularly true when the sender and receiver come from different cultures. So, what is a manager to do who has a group of employees with various cultural backgounds? The quick and easy answer is to assess your needs as a manager, the needs of the organization, then see how those fit with the needs of the employees. Where gaps exist, it is then necessary to determine how much the manager and employees need to style switch and find mutually acceptable approaches to work with each other that will support the goals of the organization. If you have done a good job of hiring people who already fit into your well-defined corporate culture, then trained them well, the friction points should be less than companies who merely hire warm bodies and throw them into the fray.

In what areas should leaders and managers strive to make adjustments with a multicultural workforce? There is no set answer to this. It depends upon the basic style of the leader, the organization's culture and the employees' needs. However, the following five areas are where there are often gaps in the intentions and perceptions of both leaders and employees, resulting in misunderstanding, miscommunication and mutual frustration.

- Conflict Resolution: A Model For Win-Win Solutions
- Meeting Management: What Does Participation Look Like?
- Team Building: Breaking Down The Walls
- Employee Motivation: Welcome The New, Keep The Existing
- Training: Not A Luxury, A Necessity

A WINDOW INTO CULTURE: PROVERBS AND SAYINGS

Language is a window into the values of a culture, and the unique proverbs and sayings used in cultures around the world are a wonderful way to explore those values. The root causes for the five areas of conflict listed above are numerous, yet many can be traced to the following fundamental values found in American culture and, thus, in the operating style of many businesses in the United States.

- Independence

- Self Sufficiency

- Assertiveness

- Egalitarian, Not Hierarchical

- Professional And Personal life-Relationships Are Transient In Nature

To show how pervasive these values are, the following section includes often used proverbs or sayings, as well as their origin. Unfortunately, these values are often directly opposed to the values held by foreign-born employees or customers, hence the friction.

There is tremendous benefit to analyzing proverbs that are commonly used in any given culture because they provide tremendous insight into the values that drive behaviors. A knowledge of the origin and meaning of proverbs used in one's own culture and the cultures of one's coworkers and customers is a way to get to know the submerged or hidden portion of your own iceberg and the icebergs of your cultural counterparts. As a leader of a multicultural team, why not incorporate an opportunity for your employees to discuss proverbs common to their respective cultures, and their meanings, as a way to build mutual understanding? In addition, if you have employees who represent the specific cultural groups of your customer base, ask them to put on their culture-coach hat and share proverbs used by your customers. It addition to being a great way to find out more about what your customers value, it can be a creative way to include your foreign-born employees in building the business.

Independence:
"God helps those who help themselves."
This is attributed to Benjamin Franklin who published it in "Poor Richard's Almanac" in 1757. The original form was, "God helps them that help themselves."[i]

Self Sufficiency:
"Pull yourself up by your own bootstraps."
The original source is unknown, yet this phrase is used to describe someone who has succeeded on their own, unaided by any outside source or person. Another form of the saying is: "He raised himself by his own bootstraps."[ii]

Assertiveness:
"The squeaky wheel gets the grease."
This was originally used by the American humorist Henry Wheeler Shaw, 1818-1885. Shaw, using the pen name of Josh Billings included it in part of his poem, "The Kicker." The orignial form was, "The wheel that squeaks the loudest is the one that gets the grease".[iii]

"Speak now, or forever hold your peace."
This comes from "The Book of Common Prayer," which was derived from the "English Prayer Book" that was originally compiled in 1549. The phrase is adapted from the Solemnization of Matrimony which is: "If any man can show just cause, why they may not lawfully be joined together, let him now speak, or else hereafter for ever hold his peace." [iv]

Egalitarian, Not Hierarchical:
"All men are created equal."
Thomas Jefferson, Declaration of Independence, July 4, 1776.[v]

Professional And Personal
Life-Relationships Are Transient In Nature:
"Go west, young man."
Originally penned by John B.L. Soule and published in the "Terra Haute Express" in 1851. However, the phrase was made popular by and widely attributed to Horace Greeley, who expanded on the expression in an editorial in the New York Tribune in 1851. Greeley's editorial said: "Go west, young man, and grow up with the country." If you consider the time this phrase was originally used, it is easy to see how the prevalent value in the United States at the time was to move on, break new ground and explore new territory. The very nature of continuous movement, at that time, meant that a farmer could exhaust his land, then merely move to virgin territory to start another. In other words, it could be interpreted that one could easily move away from his or her problems; There were plenty of options. Fast forward to the business environment of today and it isn't too hard to see the similarities: People change jobs

and even careers on a regular basis. A failure in one company or career can be a standout in another. Why worry about relationships if the players on the team are likely to change anyway?[vi]

CULTURAL FRICTION: FROM MODELS OF FAILURE TO MODELS OF SUCCESS

Let's take a look at how problems start, and how they can be resolved in each of the five common areas of cultural friction. Of course, it takes two to create the friction and misunderstandings, and both sides have their own points of view. Unless both sides take the time to analyze each others' intentions and perceptions, neither will know if or how much to style switch, and the cycle of misunderstanding is bound to continue. To help clarify this, the five conflict areas are analyzed in the following order:

- The conflict area is summarized, then two scenarios are included to illustrate actual incidents:

A) The Problem: Actual Scenario 1
B) The Solution to Actual Scenario 1
C) The Problem: Actual Scenario 2
D) The Solution to Actual Scenario 2

Each of the two scenarios is divided into two parts: the problem and the solution. The first part, identified as the problem, represents failure. It introduces comments made my disgruntled, foreign-born employees about their North

American managers or colleagues. These represent work environments where cultural differences are, at worst, not recognized and, at least, not dealt with in a constructive manner: The result is miscommunication and frustration. The second set, identified as the solution, represents success. It contains comments made by satisfied foreign-born employees who appreciate the steps their managers or colleagues have taken to accommodate their linguistic or cultural needs. In many cases, both the management and foreign-born employees have taken the time to develop mutually acceptable approaches after clarifying expectations and frustrations.

All comments were made by employees who work in a variety of companies and industries in North America, from book stores, fast-food restaurants and video stores, to hospitals, vacation resorts, high-tech firms and factories.

It is important to note the section that comes immediately after each "Problem Scenario" and before each "Solution Scenario." This section lists the negative perceptions the employee and leader had of each other, the positive intentions each had, then what they expect of each other (how they want the other to style switch) in order to create a more acceptable work environment. Direct quotes from the employees and managers involved in the scenarios are categorized as shown below:

Employee's Perception Of Manager (negative): This is the employee's critical view of the approach the manager took.

Employee's Intention (positive): What the employee intended to do which, when viewed from his or her cultural common sense, is entirely positive.

Employee's Expectation (of manager): This details to what extent the employee wants the manager to style switch in order to be more effective with people from the employee's home culture.

Manager's Perception Of Employee (negative): This is the manager's critical view of the behavior of the employee.

Manager's Intention (positive): What the manager or leader intended to do which, when viewed from his or her cultural common sense, is entirely positive.

Manager's Expectation (of employee): This details to what extent the manager would like the employee to style switch in order to be more effective with managers and co-workers who are either from North America or are used to doing business in North America.

THE SCENARIOS

Which set best reflects how your foreign-born employees interact with their managers or colleagues?

1) CONFLICT RESOLUTION

Conflict is inevitable in any team; there is no getting around it. Even teams comprised of people who have the same cultural background, come from the same state or province, or even the same town will eventually have to solve some sort of conflict. If teams of people from the same culture can have difficulty, then multicultural teams are not only guaranteed to have conflict, but more of it, over seemingly mundane issues. That is, of course, unless the leader and team members strive to style switch in mutually acceptable ways; They have to create the hybrid culture that was described in chapter two. It is imperative that multucultural teams discuss both the sources of frustration, then how to avoid or deal with them *before* the team embarks on its task. It's like making marriage counseling *during* the honeymoon mandatory for newlyweds, when minds are flexible and open, before their culturally driven communication styles, values and common senses cause problems. If this is done, the multicultural team can actually be a stronger, more creative and more cohesive unit than its monocultural cousins.

Good leaders of monocultural teams don't necessarily need to identify, in advance, the irritations that can grow into the kind of strife that has the potential to tear teams apart. Nor do they necessarily need to think of, in advance, how to resolve such conflict. Why? Because in monocultural teams, there is probably a similarity of values and common sense that influence *what* becomes a problem and *how* to solve it. This is particularly true in organizations with well-defined and articulated corporate cultures; people wouldn't join the organization in the first place if they didn't buy into the way business was done.

A) Conflict Resolution - The Problem
Scenario #1

"My manager is so insensitive. I told him I had a problem with one of my co-workers and he said I should talk it over with that person directly. If that didn't work, then I should tell him and he would give me some specific suggestions for how to approach my co-worker. When I told him I wasn't comfortable with that, he told me that he `didn't have time to babysit a bunch of employees who should work things out alone.` Back in my home culture, the manager would act as a go-between and actively help solve the problem."

Employee's Perception Of Manager (negative): "My manager isn't doing his job. I am not a `baby` and I resent that choice of words."

Employee's Intention (positive): "I want to take care of the problem I am having with my co-worker but don't know how to do it in the direct style my manager suggests. I don't want to cause additional problems with my co-worker, so I asked my manager to be a go-between."

Employee's Expectation (of manager): "In my home culture, a manager takes a very active role in making sure employees are getting along. It is not uncommon for the manager to solve problems between employees, and the employees never have to discuss the issue directly. Sometimes, saving face and maintaining a good relationship means the manager listens to each employee's complaints, then offers suggestions to each as to how to solve the situation. I need my manager to be a good relationship coach."

Manager's Perception Of Employee (negative): "I can't stand it when an employee complains about another, then expects me to solve the problem. I need to concentrate on the business."

Manager's Intention (positive): "Anyone who has been around a while knows that shuttle diplomacy doesn't have lasting, positive results. My strategy in this and every case of employee conflict is to put the monkey on their backs. I know it is difficult, but by directly confronting their issues, their problem will get resolved more quickly and they will grow as employees."

Manager's Expectation (of employee): "Don't bring me problems without solutions. Of course, there will be situations when I need to step in, but that is only after the employees have done their best to work things out directly. I need my staff to take the initiative and act independently of me with these types of issues."

B) Conflict Resolution - The Solution
Scenario #1

"I really appreciate my manager. I told him I had a problem with one of my female co-workers, whom I thought was overly aggressive and didn't respect me. I come from a culture where women are not as assertive and I am still not comfortable with how things are done here. My manager took the time to listen to the situation, which of course was only my side of the story. My co-worker was born and raised in this country, as was my manager, so my manager attempted to explain what values my co-worker probably had and how those affected her behavior. He asked me a number of questions about my own culture and my values. Our discussion helped me realize that my co-worker was most likely just being herself and that she had no sense of disrespect toward me. My manager offered to facilitate a discussion between my co-worker and me, but I don't think that will be necessary at this time. It still feels strange when a woman is so assertive toward me, but my manager's explanation helped me realize my co-worker wasn't attacking me personally, it is just a very common style in this culture."

C) Conflict Resolution - The Problem
Scenario #2

"My boss doesn't understand people from my culture. She always tells us to `feel free to come to her cubicle` with any issues we have. She says she believes in the `open door policy` and that we should never hesitate to use her as a confidant and coach. The problem is that in my culture, the boss initiates contact with the employee, not the other way around. So, there are many problems with our business and customers that she is not even aware of because the other employees from my culture won't approach her."

Employee's Perception Of Manager (negative): "My manager *lives* in her cubicle and is too distant from the team. I don't think she really cares about us or the customers because she is always busy with her computer and all of her e-mails."

Employee's Intention (positive): "I want to share information with my manager, but I feel like I would be invading her personal space if I invited myself into her cubicle. By working at my desk, I am showing her what a hard worker I am."

Employee's Expectation (of manager): "She needs to leave her cubicle and take the time to visit each of us, at our desks, several times each day. I want her to ask me how a certain project is going or how my recent meetings with customers went. I want her to demonstrate an interest in me and the others from my culture. Doesn't she see that the only employees who ever initiate contact with her are those from this culture?"

Manager's Perception of Employee (negative): "They keep information, particularly problems they are having with projects I have delegated, to themselves. Then they spring surprises on me at the last minute when I approach them to get a progress report. I guess they don't like to admit failure."

Manager's Intention (positive): "I am very careful to back up my words with actions. I say that I live by the open door policy and I mean it. Every time an employee comes to my cubicle, I will stop what I am doing, regardless of how busy I am, and engage them in a conversation. Of course, there are times when I am either under the pressure of a deadline, or the employee brings up an issue that will require a good chunk of time to discuss. In those cases, we always agree on a meeting time for later that day or week. I don't want to hound my staff with unnecessary questions. I had a boss that used to do that and it really bothered me. I vowed to stay out of my employees' sandboxes unless invited. Unfortunately, it is only the local employees who visit me."

Manager's Expectation (of employee): "Stop by my cubicle, even if it is merely to say `hello.` I promise I won't bite and we will nip a lot of problems in the bud."

D) Conflict Resolution - The Solution

Scenario #2

"My boss has learned how to work effectively with the various cultural groups in our department. For example, in the past when she delegated a task, she always said, `If you have any questions, don't hesitate to come to my cubicle.` She runs what she calls an open door policy, but none of the employees from my country would ever go to her cubicle, even when they had questions about what she wanted them to do. This caused a lot of problems and finger pointing. At first, she didn't know that some employees were more able to approach her to ask questions than others, and that much of this was determined by culture. So, she took the time to learn about the different cultural groups in this department to effectively alter how she delegates. She even approached me and asked me to explain how an effective manager in my home culture would delegate. I told her that in my culture, the boss initiates contact with the employee, not the other way around. Also, the more the boss asks about the progress on a project, the more interest he is showing. So, what is referred to as `meddling by the boss` in this culture is appreciated in my native culture. Also, what is seen as an assertive behavior by a subordinate in this culture would be viewed as being too selfish in my home culture. Therefore, employees tend to wait for the boss to approach them. My boss still tells the employees to 'feel free to come to her cubicle' with any questions we have, but she now is very good about leaving her cubicle and initiating one to one discussions with those employees who still won't approach her."

2) MEETING MANAGEMENT

Getting all members of a team to feel comfortable and participate in meetings is a challenge facing all managers and leaders. The endless number of books and training packages devoted to this subject, is testimony to the complexity of the task. And the lack of books and materials devoted to the art of running a meeting for a multicultural team make this process all the more difficult for any leader. How does the meeting leader effectively engage all members of the team, when each member might have a different common sense about appropriate meeting processes?

A) Meeting Management - The Problem
Scenario #1

"Even though I have lived in this country for 10 years, I have a hard time speaking up during staff meetings because I still feel my English is not good. There are times when I know I have a good idea, but the discussion has already moved on to a different topic by the time I have chosen the right words. I feel like an outsider even though I have worked here for almost three years."

Employee's Perception Of Manager (negative): "My manager and the team I work with don't care about what I know. If they did, they would help me by inviting me into the discussions."

Employee's Intention (positive): "I want to participate in the department meetings, but not to interrupt the flow that the manager and other employees have already created. How can

I be a more valuable member of the team?"

Employee's Expectation (of manager): "My manager needs to help me get into the meeting. I want her to ask me to join in and also to stop the other employees from interrupting me."

Manager's Perception Of Employee (negative): "He comes to our department meetings and just sits there. I know he has the technical expertise, but he doesn't speak up. He needs to step up to the plate and join the team."

Manager's Intention (positive): "I want everyone to pull their fair share on the team. I am constantly stating during the meetings that I want everyone to participate and ask questions. I have done my best to create an open, equal environment where everyone can participate."

Manager's Expectation (of employee): "I expect everyone on the team to pull their own weight. I can't read their minds, so they need to speak up. We're in a very competetive, fast-paced environment and I need quick responses from everyone."

B) Meeting Management - The Solution
Scenario #1

"Even though I have lived in this country for 10 years, I have a hard time speaking up during staff meetings because I still feel my English is not good. My manager knows this about me and does a good job of involving me during the meetings. For example, she knows it takes me extra time to choose the right words so she allows more time for me to answer. I just have to give her a certain glance as a signal, and she says something like: `Tran, do you have anything you would like to add?` By then, I have had enough time to think about the words. She also ensures that the others don't interrupt me when I am speaking, because Americans have the rude habit of always trying to finish my sentences. I appreciate her sensitivity."

C) Meeting Management - The Problem
Scenario #2

"I do not like brainstorming during meetings. It seems like a guessing game and in my country, I was taught not to speak up unless I could back up my opinion. I would rather have a private meeting with my supervisor to discuss new ideas, but when I told him, he said there wasn't enough time in a day to do so and told me to `just speak up.`"

Employee's Perception Of Manager (negative): "My manager always uses brainstorming meetings to boost creativity. He doesn't realize that I have a very hard time jumping in with ideas that are not well thought out. He has ignored my requests to have private meetings with him. He obviously doesn't value my ideas."

Employee's Intention (positive): "I want to participate in the department meetings. I have many creative ideas, but I cannot contribute them during the brainstorming meetings. I am not able to back up my opinion so I don't want to waste everyone's time with a stupid idea that I just thought of."

Employee's Expectation (of manager): "My manager should respect my cultural background and try to understand how difficult it is for me to verbalize my opinions in front of the group. I want to work with him to come up with some sort of solution to this problem."

Manager's Perception Of Employee (negative): "She really offers nothing during our brainstorming sessions, so she might as well not attend. I know she isn't used to this type of meeting style, but hey, this is how things are done in this country and she needs to get used to it."

Manager's Intention (positive): "I use brainstorming as a tool to mine the creativity of the team. She has good ideas because she has shared them with me in the past. I want our team to shine so that we all reap the benefits of increased business and bonuses. I know brainstorming works and am trying to help all members of the team realize this."

Manager's Expectation (of employee): "Participation from all."

D) Meeting Management - The Solution
Scenario #2

"I do not like brainstorming during meetings. It seems like a guessing game and in my country, I was taught not to speak up unless I could back up my opinion. Also, the pace is much too fast, so I usually don't say much. My manager told me that he noticed my silence and asked me what was wrong, so I told him. Ideally, I would have private meetings with him, but he and I agreed that there was not enough time for us to always do that, so we came up with a good compromise. Instead of always having verbal brainstorm sessions, we now have what we call `sticky tab` sessions. Instead of verbalizing our ideas, each of us writes our idea on the tabs of paper that have the self-stick backs. We then post those tabs on a flip chart at the front of the room and our manager reads them. I am more comfortable with this approach. An added benefit is that some of the other team members, who are a bit shy, like this approach as well and they don't even have the cultural issues I do."

3) TEAMBUILDING

What is a strong team? How does one go about building one? This is one of the most challenging aspects of multicultural leadership. The behaviors of members of one cultural group are easily mistaken as either too distant or too "touchy-feely" by members of other cultural groups. Striking a balance of paying personal attention to some members of a team, while keeping "out of the sandbox" of other members of a team is an art that cannot be understated in its importance for the new age of global business dealings.

A) Teambuilding - The Problem
Scenario #1

"My manager seems so cold and uncaring. In my home country, a good manager gives us greetings such as 'Good morning' at the start of the day, or 'Have a good evening' when we leave at night. In addition, they often take time after work to socialize with employees to develop good relationships. My manager rarely gives a greeting, unless I say something first, then disappears after work to spend time with her family. She did provide a couple of teambuilding activities through the training division, but they were too formal. We just need to talk more. I am trying to understand her approach, but I don't like it."

Employee's Perception Of Manager (negative): "My manager is cold, distant and doesn't care about us. It's everybody for themselves."

Employee's Intention (positive): "I want to have a strong team and one way to do that is to have a good relationship with my manager and co-workers. I don't want to be a problem, so I haven't said anything to her."

Employee's Expectation (of manager): "It is the responsibilty of the manager to create the team. She needs to socialize with us more. She could greet us in the morning and evening and could even spend time having casual discussions with us after work instead of rushing home every day."

Manager's Perception Of Employee (negative): "What is the issue with all of this relationship stuff? Of course, I want to have a strong team, so I have organized teambuilding activities through our training department. I am their manager, not their friend. What more do they want?"

Manager's Intention (positive): "I need to maintain a balance between my obligations at work and with my family. I have two young children, so I don't have a lot of flexibility to socialize in the evenings. I thought the teambuilding sessions the training department organized were enough."

Manager's Expectation Of Employee: "Honest feedback from the team. I need to have an open discussion to clarify what the group identifies as strategies to build a strong team."

B) Teambuilding - The Solution
Scenario #1

"People from this culture typically go home right after work and rarely socialize with each other. Of course, there is a golf league and basketball league, and the usual summer and winter company parties, but not much else. My manager knows that many of us on the staff are from different cultures in which developing personal relationships with co-workers and supervisors are quite important. She has her own family, so she can't participate in a lot of after hours activities with us. To make up for that, she had individual discussions with each of member of the team to determine how to build personal relationships. The result is that she tries to balance her personal needs and our need for time with her. In some cases, she invites members of the team to join her at the employee cafeteria for coffee, and some evenings she stays only 30 minutes later than her usual time to join us for small talk. She has also been very good at saying hello to us in the mornings. I used to be so careful not to interrupt her when I left in the evenings, so I never said goodbye to her. But, after our discussion, I know she appreciates our greetings as well, so I make go by her cubicle when I leave in the evening to say goodbye. I appreciate her effort."

C) Teambuilding - The Problem
Scenario #2

"I usually go to lunch with colleagues who come from my home country. It's not that I don't like the local employees; there just doesn't seem to be a good way to invite myself into their lunch groups. I am afraid that my English isn't good enough to keep up and, since they never invite me to lunch, I assume they don't want to get to know me. Even though we are all part of the same department, we really have no connection as a team and I think the lack of communication leads to a lack of trust and much frustration. When you go to the cafeteria, it is quite common to see separate tables of people from that culture alone. It is a shame we don't interact more."

Employee's Perception Of Manager(negative): "My co-workers who are from this country exclude those of us who are foreign-born. We have nothing in common. If you don't speak perfect English, you are left out."

Employee's Intention (positive): "A team should be like a family. We need to share both business and personal information to create a strong bond. My English is very poor, so I am afraid to join the native speakers of English. I don't approach them because I don't want to bother them."

Employee's Expectation Of Manager: "The head of the department should be aware of these issues. I don't think it should be up to me to force myself onto the other co-workers. The department head needs to help the employees communicate better and provide opportunities for us to form a strong team."

Manager's Perception (negative): "I had no idea my foreign-born employees had an issue with lunchtime groups. I have my hands full taking care of the business, do I also have to be the social director?"

Manager's Intention (positive): "If I forced the employees at my former company to go to lunch in certain groups, they would have thought I was meddling in their business. I have always tried to separate business time and personal time. I don't want to be an autocratic leader."

Manager's Expectation Of Employee: "My hope is that they would work through the personal issue on their own, but if they expect more direction from me, they have to let me know, I can't read their minds."

D) Teambuilding - The Solution
Scenario #2

"Those of us from foreign countries used to eat lunch only with others from our country. Including the North American employees, we have at least six different cultures represented in this department. It was comfortable to relax by speaking in our native language and, besides, none of the people from this country invited us to join their tables for lunch. Our division director noticed this and began asking us if we were comfortable with the way things were, or if there was a creative way to use the lunch hour to get to know each other. After he talked with most of the staff, he suggested we start a weekly culture appreciation day. For the last year, all of us in the dapartment have used the lunch hour on two Fridays per month to share our cultural backgrounds with each other. We assign a week when those from a particular culture have the responsibility of preparing some sort of native dish for the others. Of course, we all bring our own lunches, so there is not a lot of pressure to cook a lot of food. Then, during lunch, members of the 'host' culture for that day share something about their culture. Sometimes it is nothing more than teaching the rest of the group a traditional song or dance. At other times, however, the hosts explain something about their history, religion or native art. Some of us even bring in some sort of decorations and wear examples of our native clothing to make it more fun. It has been a tremendous opportunity to get to know each other and build a strong team. As a result, we are more comfortable with each other, and often have lunch and interact with other cultural groups every day of the week. It has resulted in much more useful communication during the day as well. We often share strategies each other about how to most effectively deal with customers who come from our different cultural groups."

4) MOTIVATION

So, the team is put together. Now, how do you keep everyone on the team motivated? For the manager or leader who has limited exposure to working with multicultural teams, this can be one of the most vexing problems to face and correct. This is because virtually every area of management common sense is up for grabs when it comes to motivating a workforce made up of people from different cultures. A strategy that has served a manager well for years can suddenly be the reason his or her team is now falling apart. As with any of these five conflict areas, it is critically important for the manager of a multicultural team to utilize culture coaches to help determine an appropriate approach when considering motivation strategies and programs.

A) Motivation - The Problem
Scenario #1

"I am not comfortable with the employee of the month award. I was given the award one month and was ashamed that my picture was posted in the store. In my home culture, the team is everything and the individual is just a part of the team, and having my picture up made me feel arrogant. When I asked my manager to take the picture down, he just laughed and said I should be proud of my accomplishment. I know he meant well, but I was very uncomfortable."

Employee's Perception Of Manager (negative): "The store manager *assumes* that this program helps motivation. Well, it might work for the employees from this culture, but not for me. He doesn't care to find out other ways to raise motivation. Once again, it is up to me to bend and fit into this culture, even though five of the 15 employees in this store are not originally from this culture."

Employee's Intention (positive): "First, I don't want to appear selfish or self-centered to my co-workers. That is why I asked my manager to take my picture down. Second, we have a very diverse employee group in this store and I think we could do so much more to improve motivation. I was hoping I could have a good discussion with my manager about alternative motivation programs, but he won't listen."

Employee's Expectation Of Manager: "I have a right to request my picture not be posted, but he didn't seem to care. He needs to listen to me and the rest of us who come from outside this country."

Manager's Perception Of Employee (negative): "I don't understand how something as positive as this program can get turned into something so negative. If I adjusted the rewards program to meet the needs of every individual employee, I'd probably anger more people plus I wouldn't get any work done."

Manager's Intention (positive): "Recognition of my employees' accomplishments is a positive thing. I have used this approach for the last 25 years and it has never been a problem before."

Manager's Expectation Of Employee: "Appreciate what I am doing for them. They don't know how good they have it here. I just want a content, motivated team that works well together and celebrates when we have a good month."

B) Motivation - The Solution
Scenario #1

"My manager knows that I am not comfortable with the employee of the month award. Every month, the employee with the most sales is rewarded by having his or her picture and name posted on the wall behind the cash register. When I told him I was uncomfortable, he asked me why I had a problem with it. I explained to him that in my home culture, the team is everything and the individual is just a part of the team. I also told him that a number of other employees aren't comfortable with the present system. He asked me what would be more appropriate. I told him that I knew the employees from this country really liked the program and that it is part of this culture, so perhaps we could just put my name up and not my picture. I suggested that this might work with some of the other non-native employees and he told me he would talk to them. He promised me he would also talk with the employees are from this local culture and explain the situation so they would understand. He said he hopes to gather a number of ideas from all of the employees, then rotate the various motivation strategies on a monthly basis. I appreciate his flexibility."

C) Motivation - The Problem
Scenario #2

"The performance review system of this company is so impersonal. My supervisor meets with me two times in a year to go over my strengths and weaknesses. Besides those formal meetings, I rarely hear from her. And when we do meet, she is always in such a rush to finish. I can't gather my thoughts so quickly in English, so she does most of the talking. In my country, supervisors and employees spend a lot of time together; we eat lunch together, play cards during breaks and share personal information. Of course, during those times, our supervisors often give us information about how we are doing on the job. Two rushed meetings a year is not enough."

Employee's Perception Of Manager (negative): "My supervisor doesn't care about the employees. Even when we meet, she is so busy that we only have 30 to 45 minutes to talk. Of course, she does most of the talking … this is so typical in this culture. Whoever talks the most has the 'best' ideas and I don't like it."

Employee's Intention (positive): "I want to improve as an employee. I came to this country to get chances that I can't get back home. My plan is to continually improve both my English and my technical skills in this department. I need more time with my supervisor to do this. She has many years of experience in this area and I want to learn from her."

Employee's Expectation Of Manager: "I want her to give me more of her time and train me. She should take the time to meet us outside the official performance review times. It would be very nice if she learned something about my culture so we can have a more effective relationship. I would also appreciate her not interrupting me when I am still talking."

Manager's Perception Of Employee (negative): "We have a very progressive compensation package compared to our competitors, so what are they complaining about? I always tell my team that I'm available should they need me. How can they criticize me about the lack of time I spend with them when they don't approach me?"

Manager's Intention (positive): " I give the same amount of time to each employee and always make myself available to those who request more time with me. I don't want to be accused of playing favorites, so I treat everyone the same."

Manager's Expectation Of Employee: "Be honest with me. If I am doing something wrong, let me know. Also, I have many other responsibilities fighting political battles, so realize that I can't always be around."

D) Motivation - The Solution
Scenario #2

"The official performance review system of this company is so impersonal. It merely requires a supervisor to meet with employees two times in a year to go over strengths and weaknesses. Many supervisors do little more than that when it comes to communicating with employees. Luckily, my supervisor has worked in several other countries and realizes there are many ways to do preformance reviews. When I was first hired, she explained the company policy and what was required. To my surprise, she then asked me to explain how performance reviews were conducted in my home country and what I preferred. It took about an hour, but she and I eventually decided upon a strategy that would give me what I expected from a boss and enabled her to give the company what it required. In addition to the weekly staff meetings, she and I initially met once a week for a one-to-one meeting, for 15 minutes at most. We met regardless of what was going on and even if I didn't have any problems. After my first six months on the job, we reduced these meetings to once every two weeks. By then, we had become comfortable with each other so we didn't need to rely on scheduled meetings to get together. I was able to go to her office if I had a question and she would often stop by my desk just to chat. Since I was more relaxed, my English also improved. By the end of the first year, we were so used to each other's styles, that we cancelled the one-to-one meetings. It's funny, though; we still manage to meet when we need to. Now, when we meet for the six-month preformance review, it truly is a review. It took some time, but the outcome was a true win-win scenario."

5) TRAINING

There are two distinct issues regarding training in a company attempting to provide global customer service. The first issue, and this is found in any number of companies, is there are tremendous pressures to minimize or eliminate training programs in an effort to cut costs and get employees out to the front lines as quickly as possible. "I don't have the budget or the time to train my staff" is a common complaint voiced by leaders and managers in companies both large and small. The second issue is unique to companies that already have or plan to have a multicultural staff to handle their diverse customers. They don't take the cultural needs of their employees into account when designing or implementing training programs. Not all adult learners are comfortable with the student-centered model of instruction so regularly used in American-based companies. For this model to work, the following assumptions must apply to the trainees:

- They understand English, written as well as spoken.
- In addition to understanding English, they can interact in English. This means that they are comfortable asking questions, challenging the instructor and co-trainees

during class and can hold their own in the fast-paced environment of so many training programs.

A) Training - The Problem
Scenario #1

"I recently attended a customer service training session. The trainer was very knowledgeable about giving good service to customers who were born in this country, but he didn't know the first thing about dealing with people from my country. This company has a lot of customers who emigrated from my country, but most employees don't know how to treat them appropriately. During the training session, I tried to share some of my thoughts, but the trainer didn't seem interested. It is hard enough for me to communicate in English, then when the trainer told me to save my thoughts for later, I felt insulted."

Employee's Perception Of Manager/Trainer (negative): "The trainer was rude and didn't even listen to me. When he told me to save my thought for later, I thought he was telling me to shut up and I was shocked. I felt like I would have had to stand on the table and scream to be heard by him. He was as rude to me as many employees in this company are to customers who come from my culture."

Employee's Intention (positive): "The company is so good to provide us with customer service training. Unfortunately, a large population of our foreign customers was not even addressed during the program. I wanted to add some ideas to make the training more effective, but since he didn't want listen to me the first time, I didn't feel like getting into an argument when he asked me for my opinion later."

Employee's Expectation Of Trainer: "The company and training staff should welcome new ideas and be glad that I was trying to offer suggestions instead of ignoring me. They need to design a new class that provides education about other cultures, not just this one."

Trainer's Perception Of Employee(negative): "How can he complain about the training? This was the first I had heard of the cultural issues he was bringing up in the middle of class. I told him I would be happy to discuss some of his issues later during the session, but when I came back to him, he clammed up. I knew he had some comments, but there is only so much I can do as a facilitator."

Trainer's Intention (positive): " I *was* interested in his comments about his culture and told him so. I even said that I wanted to hear more about his ideas later, but at that moment, we were in the middle of a completely different topic. So, I used a common trainer's response and asked him to hold his thought for later when I could give it more attention. I even wrote his comment on the flip chart pad so I wouldn't forget to ask later. What I did is considered good facilitation…at least in this culture. I did not intend to ignore him or minimize his concerns."

Trainer'sExpectation Of Participants: "Speak up. Take care of your own learning content and pace. I have an average of 15 participants per class and we always clarify the ground rules before training. One of them is, all participate. All he

had to do was let me know. As a child I learned the proverb
`Speak now, or forever hold your peace.` I believe in it and
design my training classes by it."

B) Training - The Solution
Scenario #1

"This company is very good at taking care of our multicultural employees and customers. As an example, several weeks before I attended a recent customer service
training session, the trainer approached me and asked
me for my advice about how to work effectively with
customers from my culture. She said that she had
noticed I was quiet during most meetings and training
sessions, but presumed it wasn't because I didn't have any
ideas. She told me she had read somewhere that many
people from my culture aren't comfortable speaking up
in group settings, so she wanted to have a chance to get
to know me in a one-to-one setting. She asked me some
very detailed questions about what people from my culture like or dislike when shopping for goods or services.
Because I felt at ease talking with her, I told her that
many people from my culture like to have a warm greeting from a shop employee when they enter a store. In
addition, even if we don't buy anything, we appreciate it
when the shop staff says something like, `Thank you for
shopping here today,` as we leave the store. I told her
that it might seem like a small issue, but if we trained
our store employees to do this, I had no doubt the customers from my culture would greatly appreciate it. To
my surprise, when I attended the training class, I found
that she had prepared a whole section on appropriate

greetings and salutations. To make it even more interesting, she gave examples from four different cultures
and people from those cultures are employed here and
are also our customers. She really did a good job of both
preparing the class and taking care of my preference for
one-to-one discussions over classroom discussions."

C) Training - The Problem
Scenario #2

"I don't understand the approach to employee training
in this country. Trainers usually give the participants
some general information about a problem, then ask for
comments about how we, the participants, would handle such a situation. How are we supposed to know? In
my country, the trainer or teacher gives many examples
of how to best solve the problem, then has students
practice that model over and over. I feel lost without
those models, so I never speak up during training sessions here. They probably think I am stupid."

Employee's Perception Of Manager/Trainer (negative): "The
trainer is supposed to teach us, not the other way around. Why
would he ask us for answers before he has taught us? Why
would he ask us to participate in role-plays before he showed us
the correct way? I felt put on the spot and foolish since I didn't
offer any suggestions. Also, the employees from this culture feel
free to share their strategies and, quite frankly, some of their
examples are not useful and wasted the time in class. I was very
uncomfortable and think the class was a waste of time."

Employee's Intention (positive): "To be a good student and employee. I want to learn new strategies; that is why I attend class. I don't want to share my ideas because they are probably wrong, so I want to listen and take notes."

Employee's Expectation Of Trainer: "Don't ask so many questions, or demand that we join the role-plays. Just teach and provide the students with models that are already successful. I don't care so much about the opinions of other students, I want to hear from the expert."

Trainer's Perception Of Employee (negative): "She never participates, so I don't know how much she understands. She doesn't add much to the class and I don't appreciate her reluctance to join the role-plays."

Trainer's Intention (positive): " To involve the class. I have my own ideas about successful strategies, but I think my participants do too. The last thing I want to do is stand up and lecture the class. They are adults and have a lot to offer."

Trainer's Expectation Of Participants: "I know some of the participants have extensive experience in some of the topics I teach and I want them to offer their expertise. And, even if someone doesn't have experience, I want them to *attempt* to solve a problem before I give the answers."

D) Training - The Solution
Scenario #2

"The supervisor in my store is also responsible for employee training. Before he presented a class on effective sales techniques, he was careful to ask each participant to share with him their opinion of effective teaching styles. Several of us told him that in our home culture, unlike the culture here, teachers are careful to provide models of effective behavior for the students to copy. Our home culture relies less on student interaction and more on teacher modeling. He was very understanding of our need to view a model from an expert, but he also was quite eager to hear from us about effective sales techniques in our culture. We told him that many people from our culture like to negotiate a price for a product, that we don't automatically accept the price as it appears on the tag or when the employee tells us the price. In addition, we told her that several employees in our department had already come to us asking how to handle customers from our culture who always seem to want to haggle. Our response is always the same: tell them this is the price, be firm and don't worry. Hearing this, the trainer asked us to consider participating in a role-play in front of class to demonstrate the appropriate behavior. At first, we all resisted. After all, he was the teacher. However, he suggested we practice in the privacy of his office so we wouldn't be embarrassed. We worked out a very realistic scenario and practiced it several times before we felt comfortable. The next week, we then did the role play in front of the class and it was very successful. After we did the role play, I was amazed by the large number of participants who told us they had similar problems with customers from my culture and were now releived to learn an effective strategy for interacting with them."

INTERNATIONAL LEADERSHIP AT HOME:
THINK GLOBALLY, ACT LOCALLY

It has already been established that a key challenge for companies providing global service in North America and abroad is to develop leaders who are as comfortable managing people with similar cultural backgrounds as they are managing a culturally diverse workforce. The sad truth is that many corporations in North America and around the globe do not work through cultural differences in a proactive manner. The five conflict areas already introduced in this chapter highlighted the most common areas of ignorance and friction. Unfortunately, very few companies have actually progressed to the successful solution level introduced in each of the five conflict areas. The problem areas are the overwhelming majority in most companies. Hence, it is not uncommon for their multicultural employees and customers to feel ignored, unappreciated and even belittled.

Of course there are exceptions to this statement. However, a large number of managers in North American organizations that do business internationally, or who serve a diverse group of employees and customers domestically, often fall into one of two categories: they deny culture is an issue, and refuse to talk about differences because they are concerned that the mere discussion of differences will drive their multicultural workforce apart; or they recognize it but are either afraid to tackle the issue, too busy with "more important" issues, or don't know where to begin.

The large multinational corporations that have become household names to many of us have struggled for years to develop international leaders and managers who are capable of moving from country to country with relative ease. They have invested tremendous resources to both identify, then train their international management teams. A good number of them have been extremely successful in their efforts. The strategies they employ when preparing managers and leaders for assignments in a foreign countries are applicable right here in North America, so why not learn from them?

THE INTERNATIONAL LEADERSHIP WORKSHOP

Several colleagues of mine and I have facilitated numerous international leadership workshops over the past 25 years for the management teams of many world-renowned firms. We have conducted these workshops all over the world and our audiences have included managers from every continent. Although the specific content of the workshops differs from company to company, the overriding theme is always the same: how to take a group of people who come from diverse cultural backgrounds and help them build a team that agrees upon a common goal and then creates mutually acceptable strategies for working together to achieve that goal. Of all the workshops we have conducted, one series we provided for a U.S.-based global engineering firm stands out in particular as a model of success. We provided these three-day workshops once per quarter over a three- year period and approximately 240 employees participated during this time. The participants were young, newly promoted international managers who had been identified as "fast trackers" by the firm. They came from a number of countries, including Britain, France, Iran, Canada, Germany, Pakistan, Ireland, Saudi Arabia,

Australia, Spain, India, Italy, and the United States. They had all been successful in their own countries and were being groomed to take positions as project leaders with the firm in locations other than their home countries.

Of course, one of the primary goal of the workshops was to help these managers realize the importance of being culturally sensitive when leading projects in cross-cultural situations. Their technical education and business success in their home countries was just the first step in their journey to becoming true international managers—leaders who were comfortable and effective in both monocultural and cross-cultural situations. Critical to their success, and one of the fundamentals we emphasized during all workshops, was the concept of developing one's cultural sense and not blindly relying upon the common sense that had served them so well in the past when they managed employees from their own cultures.

Each workshop averaged 20 international managers, with five to seven different countries represented in each session. In an effort to leverage the multicultural makeup of the group, we developed a variety of exercises that would help the participants learn more about the following three areas:

A) Recognition of their own cultural backgrounds and the common sense practices they had developed to be effective leaders in their home countries.

B) Through the cultural backgrounds of the other participants and examples they shared, realize the wide range of leadership approaches and practices that existed in other countries that might be totally different from what they considered effective. Specifically, to assess whether or not

their long-standing common sense approaches to leadership would hold up in the international arena.

C) Discuss and practice alternative leadership practices,
based on cultural sense, that would take into account
the needs of subordinates who came from different cultural backgrounds.

In particular, there was one group activity we had them
participate in that dramatically demonstrated the importance
of changing one's approach, to *style switch*, in order to be effective when leading employees from different cultural backgrounds. We grouped all of the participants into monocultural
teams; for example, all of the French participants at one table,
all of those from Iran at another and so on. All groups were in
the same room. Then, we assigned the following task:

*As a leader, you have one hour to counsel an employee who is hav-
ing difficulty with some aspect of his or her job. The employee is
from your home culture. Discuss in your monocultural groups how
you would handle this type of situation as a leader. Specifically,
how would you conduct a one-to-one meeting and what would
you need to do or say to ensure the session was as effective as possible? Or, if you were the subordinate, what you would expect
from your boss in this type of meeting?*

Each team had one hour to discuss, then list on large flip
chart pads their specifics for success. At the conclusion of the
first hour, each team then reported to the other teams their
conclusions. In essence, the teams were sharing with each
other their respective *common sense* thoughts about leader-

ship....and the results were eye-opening.

An extremely clear pattern evolved during each session and it was this: the monocultural teams of Americans consistently appeared, *to the other teams*, as minimizing the importance of developing and maintaining personal relationships with their employees. Even the fellow North American teams from Canada expressed more interest in the personal side of the business. It is not that American leaders don't value relationships; they do, but in comparison to the other cultural groups, the Americans came across as cold and extremely distant. In predictable fashion, the Americans reported most often that for the counseling session, they would ask the employee to come to their office, whereupon they would jump almost immediately into the topic of discussion. At most, the warmup would consist of something like: "Hi Andy, I'm glad you could meet with me. There are a few things I think we need to discuss..." From this point, the leader then gets into the "meat" of the discussion without, in the words of many, "beating around the bush." This is because if there is too much of a warmup, say, more than a minute, it could cause the employee undue stress, wondering why the boss had called the meeting in the first place. This would continue until the last few moments of the meeting, when the leader concludes with some generic words of support such as, "You're a valued member of this team and I know you can do it. Let me know if I can be of any help." Indeed, the American teams tended to mirror the collective *common sense* so prevalent in the United States during the past 25 years, namely the importance of focusing on the *issue*, and not so much on the *person*. In fact, many leaders in the United States can probably remember the mantra so often repeated during supervisory or leadership seminars they attended earlier in their careers: "When giving feedback, especially critical, it is important to separate the issue from the person. It is not that you dislike the employee, you don't like the employee's actions and you need to focus on those behaviors." Finally, in line with the task orientation of many Americans, most American teams stated that, in the first place, they would not need a full hour with an employee unless it was a huge issue, lest they waste valuable time.

In direct contrast to the time-is-money approach of the Americans were the responses from the other monocultural groups. They tended to be focused a lot more on a balance of attending to both the *person,* and the *issue.* For example, it was not uncommon for the groups representing India to state something like the following: "Of the one hour meeting, we would need to spend, at a minimum, the first 20 minutes engaging the employee in a casual, personal conversation. We would need to inquire about the employee's family and other personal matters before ever starting a discussion about job performance. If we didn't take the time to do this, we would be perceived as cold and uncaring and our counseling session would be a failure because they would not listen to us as we addressed the work issue." Groups from Latin America and the Middle East reported similar strategies. The Europeans, while not devoting as much time as these groups, still spent much more time than the Americans on the relationship-building portion of the meeting. Indeed, this activity was not intended as an emprical study of cultural differences or similarities. To be sure, even amongst the monocultural groups, differences of opinion arose based upon a variety of factors, including age of participants, gender, geographic region where they were raised in their country, experience living, studying or working abroad and a host of other variables. The wide variety of cultural influences that were introduced in chapter two were alive and quite apparent during these sessions. Yet, when presssed to come to a consensus at their tables, the groups shared the aforementioned patterns for counseling a subordinate.

Of course, the purpose of this activity wasn't to disparage any one group or hold up other groups as models of leadership excellence. On the contrary, it was designed to allow the members of each culture to reflect upon what worked in their own cultures, and why, and to compare it to the other cultures in the room. The Indian, Middle Eastern and Latin American leaders learned that their emphasis on relationship building could be a severe detriment when managing many Americans or anyone who had grown accustomed to a more bottom-line orientation to business; they could be perceived, as one Canadian put it, "as inefficient chatterboxes who never get to the bottom line." Many of the North Americans, in particular those from the United States, learned that compared to most of the other countries represented, they came across as "cold-hearted efficiency freaks who are always in a rush and don't care about the team."

"LET'S BE FRIENDS"
MEETS "BUSINESS IS BUSINESS"

I'll never forget a completely different situation that reinforced this difference in relationship and task orientation. I was conducting a training session for a group of Saudi Arabian and Japanese managers who had been hired by a major American computer company. The company had hired them to run their operations in Saudi Arabia and Japan as managers. They were in the United States for an extended, one-year training program and a team of colleagues and I had them for the first eight weeks of this assignment. We were charged with preparing them to be effective in their positions as filters between the rough-and-tumble U.S. headquarters and their offices in Japan and Saudi Arabia. Polishing their English was a small portion of the curriculum. We found our greatest challenge was preparing them to be more assertive, to speak their minds during meetings and to recognize and deal with the inherent differences in management styles between U.S.-based companies and companies in their countries.

One part of the curriculum was to invite American executives from the headquarters to the training center to interact with the Saudi and Japanese trainees. This came both at the beginning and end of the eight-week training program. The memorable interaction I observed came at the end of one of the training programs and occurred in a meeting between three American executives and some of the Saudi and Japanese managers. One of the Saudi managers stated that he was homesick for the personal interaction that so often occurred back home. He talked about how commonplace it was to socialize after work with his colleagues and how they would spend hours drinking coffee and discussing any number of current events. He said that he was looking forward to developing friendships with the American executives once he arrived at headquarters because, he stated, "We will be working together for a long time and I like working with friends." Hearing this, the Americans looked puzzled and one replied, "We are not here to be your friends. This is just business." You could have heard a pin drop. I imagine so.

Certainly, there are plenty of examples of Americans who do become friends with co-workers and spend a lot of time outside the office socializing. Yet the norm in the United States is to separate work time and personal time, just as it is common to separate the issue from the person when giving critical feedback.

ACT LIKE A MULTINATIONAL MANAGER, AT HOME

So, what does all of this mean to the manager or leader who doesn't ever leave Canada or the United States? Plenty. In fact, it is the whole premise of this book. The question posed at the beginning of chapter one states it all: *The world is shrinking. Is your business expanding?* Even for those companies that don't expand beyond their nation's borders, the number of foreign-born customers and employees they come into contact with will only increase. Thus, the lessons that thousands of international managers have learned over the years about managing effectively across cultures are becoming fundamentals for success *at home*. Most likely, you are reading this book because you are a leader in a company that already recognizes this and want to excel in the ever expanding global economy.

There are a variety of leadership styles that can be utilized and the leader of an intercultural team needs to have the abilty to *style switch* to bring out the best from his or her staff. Over the years, the managers who have participated in our international leadership workshops have learned about and practiced the strategy of using a culture coach to help determine how, to what extent and when to *style switch*. In fact, throughout every workshop, we have the participants divide into a number of culturally diverse breakout teams to take advantage of the cultural knowledge present in the group. We always have a room full of culture coaches, so why not take advantage of them? Once in the culturally diverse teams, we assign different tasks and the participants are required to rotate the role of leader, so each has the challenge of leading the team through a task. Tasks range from simple group games and intergroup competitions to survival exercises and putting together elaborate puzzles. The tasks are designed as mediums to create opportunities for interaction, tension, conflict and resolution, and each leader and team is graded on their performance. When given the role of leader for a specific task, every participant knows the only way to fully leverage the knowledge of all members of his or her breakout group is to determine a leadership approach that works for everyone. This requires the leader to take the time to literally interview individual members to determine how they want to be led or managed. Due to the multicultural nature of these teams, the accomodations the leaders and participants make to work together effectively are often numerous and run the gamut from rather simple to complex.

Quite simply, the leaders and participants in all of these exercises eventually came to grips with some fundamental approaches and attitudes regarding multicultural effectiveness. As outlined in chapter two, there are a number of essential principles and approaches one can take to ensure success with members of different cultures. However, the following two are key for any leader and resonated strongly with our seminar participants:

- Cultural self-awareness and cultural other-awareness are critical tools for enhancing effectiveness.
  Get to know your own culturally determined likes and dislikes (your own iceberg) while studying the likes and dislikes of your multicultural customers and employees.

- Different cultures and different personalities require different approaches; be flexible, since no single strategy, tactic or procedure always works.

As an example, here are some of the most common ways the teams and leaders have *style switched* over the years in our workshops to create those strong teams:

Speak Slowly. If English was the default language, the native speakers had to agree to speak slowly and avoid using regional slang or colloquial expressions. Non native-English speakers recognized that their accents made their English harder to understand when they spoke rapidly, so the same rules applied to them.

Use Visual Support. Verbal exchanges had the potential of excluding some of the particpants, especially those who had a harder time listening to or expressing themselves in English, or the default language. So the use of flip charts, models, or actual demonstrations of concepts were encouraged to keep all engaged.

Encourage Native-Language Sub Discussions. When two or more members of a breakout group were from the same culture, or shared a common language other than English or the agreed-upon default language, time was allotted for them to gather in sub-groups to clarify concepts and help each other out. This was not considered a waste of time. In fact, some groups actually included this "native language discussion time" in their meeting agendas to ensure all members were given ample opportunity to participate.

Develop Ground Rules For Interaction. Decide *before* a meeting or conference the group processes that will enable maximum participation from all. How often should native language sub discussions be scheduled? Will verbal exchanges such as brainstorming be balanced with written exchanges or more private one-to-one exchanges? How will decisions be made, then enforced? This process is a crucial step to ensure all team members have the chance to express their views, and "be heard".

Assign "Gatekeepers." Once the ground rules and processes have been decided, they need to be followed. By assigning people the role of gatekeeper, you will be putting a vital safety net in place. The gatekeepers act as process monitors to keep the group from wandering too far from agreed-upon approaches. For example, if the group agrees to brainstorm for 10 minutes of a 90-minute meeting, the gatekeepers will not only monitor the time, but they can also help all members participate. If the more vocal members of the team are dominating a discussion, the gatekeepers can act as "traffic cops" to slow down some members and speed up others.

Debrief Every Meeting. Meetings can be viewed as a micro-cosm of a company; if a company tends to have an autocratic corporate culture, you can bet most of the meetings will reflect that flavor. Assess and rate meetings using two criteria:

1) The process: How well did the participants interact?

2) The content: What business goals were attained?

Building a few minutes of debrief into the agenda of every meeting will ensure neither the process nor the content take a back seat to your efforts to build and maintain a strong multicultural team.

Celebrate Success. Have fun! Just be sure to celebrate in a way that doesn't alienate any cultural or ethnic groups. Instead of relying upon the same old worn out patterns of celabrating that have taken place in the past (Friday afternoon beer and pizza parties at the local watering hole), why not be creative? Ask the members of the team what they would appreciate, then alter how, when and where you kick up your heels.

Does this mean that all employees from different cultures will want special treatment? No. It is incumbent on the leader to determine how much he or she should style switch with any given employee. And the best way to determine that is to ask questions. Ask the employees directly, or ask the culture coach-es who know about the target culture or who know the employ-ee. It is entirely possible that many employees from foreign cul-tures will have already adapted to the culture of the organiza-tion or the culture of the region. Thus, reinforcing the never-ending importance of having a clearly defined corporate culture so you can create a comprehensive hiring strategy. If you hire the right people, those who will thrive in your particular corporate culture, you will have the bulk of the work behind you.

[i] Bartlett, John. *Bartlett's Familiar Quotations.* Boston: Little, Brown and Company, First Edition Published 1855, Fifteenth Edition Published 1980.

[ii] Morris, William and Mary. *Morris Dictionary of Word and Phrase Origins.* Harper Collins, 1988.

[iii] Berman, Louis A. *Proverb Wit & Wisdom: A Treasury of Proverbs, Parodies, Quips, Quotes, Cliches, Catchwords, Epigrams, and Aphorisms.* Perigree, 1997.

[iv] Berman, Louis A. *Proverb Wit & Wisdom: A Treasury of Proverbs, Parodies, Quips, Quotes, Cliches, Catchwords, Epigrams, and Aphorisms.* Perigree, 1997.

[v] Bartlett, John. *Bartlett's Familiar Quotations.* Boston: Little, Brown and Company, First Edition Published 1855, Fifteenth Edition Published 1980.

[vi] Barnett, Alex. *The Quotable American.* The Lyons Press, 2002.

CHAPTER SEVEN

YOU HAVE THE GLOBE IN YOUR HANDS: DO SOMETHING!

You now have a choice. Take the words and ideas presented in this book and put them into practice, or shelve them. Implementing change in an organization is a lot of work, yet if the change is the right one, it will make a tremendous difference in your ability to survive. And it doesn't mean that you have to be the leader of a team or an organization to implement change. The leaner and flatter organizations of today benefit from the ideas and involvement of all employees. People believe the message they get from the tone we set in our organizations. The tone or corporate culture is created through our leadership approach, honesty, and actions, not merely through pronouncements, words or motivational posters. Your words are useless unless your actions or leadership style are sending the same message.

WORDS, TONE, ACTIONS, OR, HOW SINCERE ARE YOU?

Your Spoken Words

For example: Do you or your managers say you need to be more innovative and creative, yet never try new approaches? Define "innovative" in your organization.

Your Written Words

For example: Do you sing the praises of diversity, multiculturalism and being the "employer of choice" in your mission statements or other corporate literature, yet stifle new ideas with outmoded policies or approaches?

Your Teamwork Environment (Actions)

When problems or misunderstandings arise between employees, do managers and employees use a collaborative process to discuss the problem and resolve it rather than assigning blame and creating interpersonal or intercultural friction? Do you follow up as you promise?

Set the tone of sincerity by taking action and implementing the changes that will make your team or organization more adaptable to the cultural demands of the global economy. You have the globe in your hands. Now do something!

THE WORLD IS CHANGING. ARE YOU?

Many companies and organizations embark on new initiatives to improve any number of things, including their service, product quality, production methods and leadership. However, the sad reality is that is that too many fail in their attempts. All too often, these change initiatives are started with much fanfare and public pronouncements, yet end up in the ever-growing junk pile of "flavor of the month" programs. What might have been an inherently good initiative loses popular or corporate support and falls into the category of a waste of time and money; someone's "kick," spending run amok. Within a few months, the old attitudes and destructive behavior patterns return.

Change in and of itself is not difficult. The challenge is in sustaining the change and weaving it into the corporate culture. To embark on a journey of sustained change requires answering two vital questions:

- It is the right change?

- Are support systems and supportive people in place to give it a chance to succeed?

Certainly, there are many subsections to each these questions; life is never this simple. With that said, it is important to avoid making any process too cumbersome to implement, much less sustain.

The four exercises that follow will lead you through a variety of steps to help you and your organization avoid this normal backsliding by helping answer these two questions: Is the change you need to implement the right change? And what will you put into place to ensure it has a fighting chance to succeed? The exercises will enable you and your employees or co-workers to analyze your circumstances, then identify specific action steps to ensure you move beyond discussion into implementation. In his most recent book, Warren Bennis, the founding chairman of the Leadership Institute at the University of Southern California, and author of numerous books on leadership and change, identifies *adaptive capacity* as one of the traits that allows individuals and organizations to survive and thrive during times of challenge and change[1]. He suggests leaders fail due to their inability to adapt to changing circumstances.

Well, this whole book is about changing circumstances and how to deal with them. The globe is essentially shrinking. As a result, now more than ever before, providers of goods and services have access to groups of culturally diverse customers who can have unique needs. Now, more than ever before, organizations and companies are populated by employees with diverse cultural and linguistic backgrounds.

With this said, it is entirely possible that you and your team might determine the cost benefits for altering a product, service or policy, to make it more culturally acceptable, don't justify the expense. That's your business and that's fine. We cannot be all things to all people and chasing after and trying to please too many of them can be a recipe for failure. However, after conducting some of the exercises and considering the concepts introduced in this book, my hope is that you will make these tough choices from a position of cultural awareness, not cultural ignorance.

The common sense reality that we have grown accustomed to in our business lives is under intense pressure to change. Current and future business circumstances will demand a more appropriate cultural sense from all of us. So, the question remains: are you and your organization in a position to make the changes required to take care of the needs of your multicultural customers and employees? As you read in the case studies in chapter four, the approaches can range from relatively simple and low cost, to incredibly complex. And as you saw in the case studies, individuals and organizations that adapt to the changing circumstances can reap tremendous benefits. Where do you stand?

1) What Forces Are Driving Change In Your Business?

Of all the demands from our customers and employees, the nagging question remains: what to change? One of the biggest challenges facing organizations today is knowing how, to what extent and when to adapt products, policies or service strategies that take into account the unique language or cultural needs their customers. Before implementing on a any sort of change, it is important to assess your business climate. An unfocused campaign of change, just for the sake of change, is doomed to fail.

List the variety of forces that have affected your profession in the past, those affecting you now and those in the future. For example: **A)** What did your customers expect from you four to five years ago? **B)** What do they demand today? and, **C)** What will they be asking for four to five years from now? Another question to answer focuses on what your employees expected in the past, what they expect today and what you think they will want in the future.

4-5 Years Ago	Today	4-5 Years From Now
_____	_____	_____
_____	_____	_____
_____	_____	_____
_____	_____	_____
_____	_____	_____
_____	_____	_____
_____	_____	_____
_____	_____	_____
_____	_____	_____
_____	_____	_____
_____	_____	_____
_____	_____	_____
_____	_____	_____
_____	_____	_____
_____	_____	_____
_____	_____	_____

2) Adapting To Change: How Do You Rate?

Now, using the information you just gathered about the forces of change driving your business, assess your ability to meet the needs of your customers and employees. Using a scale of one to five, rate how well you think you have done in the past, how well you are currently doing and, most important, how well _positioned_ you are to meet their needs in the future. If you have customers or employees from a variety of cultural groups, you might want to answer each set of questions several times;

Once for culture **A**, once for culture **B**, and so on. This will help you isolate culture-specific areas of success and areas requiring more attention.

Four To Five Years Ago
A. The products or services my company, division, or team delivered *in the past* met the needs of our culturally diverse customers.

Disagree		Neutral		Agree
1	2	3	4	5

Comments: _____

_____

_____

_____

_____

B. The policies and standards of my company or division *took* into account the diverse nature of our employees.

Disagree		Neutral		Agree
1	2	3	4	5

Comments: _____

_____

_____

_____

_____

Today

A. The products or services my company, division, or team *currently* deliver meet the needs of our culturally diverse customers.

Disagree		Neutral		Agree
1	2	3	4	5

Comments: _____

_____

_____

_____

_____

B. The policies and standards of my company or division take into account the diverse nature of our employees.

Disagree		Neutral		Agree
1	2	3	4	5

Comments: _____

_____

_____

_____

_____

Four To Five Years From Now

A. The products or services my company, division, or team deliver will meet the needs of our culturally diverse customers *in the future.*

Disagree		Neutral		Agree
1	2	3	4	5

Comments: _____

_____

_____

_____

_____

B. The policies and standards of my company or division are flexible enough to take into account the diverse nature of our employees *in the future.*

Disagree		Neutral		Agree
1	2	3	4	5

Comments: _____

_____

_____

_____

_____

Carefully review your results. You should be able to identify areas of strength and areas to improve upon. It is all too easy to forget about the areas of strength, those areas you identified as four and five because you're already good in those areas, so why spend more time on them? Areas hovering in the range of one and two may seem too challenging to tackle. So please don't fall into the trap of what I call the "comfort of neutrality," by focusing solely on the areas that fall nicely into the third range. They aren't too weak to bother tweaking and they are strong enough to keep functioning at acceptable levels. You need to bring the lower scores up, because they are the weak link in the long chain of service and leadership. Also, you can't ignore the areas that received strong scores, because the changing nature of the multicultural business environment will render those obsolete in no time.

3) Your Customer Service Approach: A Closer Look

This next exercise is designed to expand on exercise #2. In the previous exercise, you probably identified both successes and failures in your attempts to work across cultures with your customers or employees. You most likely gained insight about the culture of your organization and how flexible, or inflexible it is. Now, in light of your initial understanding of the service you provide these groups, elaborate on those successes and failures. What is the root cause for both and how do you maximize the successes and minimize the failures? Analyze how both you and your whole team are working together to better satisfy these customers. Ask yourself the following questions, and consider doing this as a group exercise, where you discuss these questions with your team. As with any of these exercises, the involvement of one or more culture coaches will greatly enhance the accuracy of your findings.

- What are you and your team doing that is working?
- In what areas can you and your team improve?

Each of these has four subset areas to consider: behaviors, attitudes, product or service.

Behaviors: What specific behaviors can you identify that have led to success? Is it a pattern of style switching that you or your team has adopted when dealing with a certain culture? Similarly, if there are patterns of failure, where might you adopt a different approach that is culturally acceptable?

Attitudes: Can you identify prevailing attitudes in your store, department, or organization that either lead to cultural sensitivity or a lack thereof? Attitudes are an offspring of an organization's culture and it is important to identify their origin.

Product or Service: What about your product or service appeals to your customers? What doesn't? Have you encouraged your employees, who are familiar with the cultural groups you serve, to assess whether or not what you provide is culturally appropriate? With employee groups, the service you offer might be recruiting and hiring strategies, a benefits package, or certain policies and procedures. Assess all areas where company and employee come into contact to look for areas of cultural friction.

As in the previous exercise, be sure to identify each cultural group of customers you are dealing with then ask these questions for each group. Then, notice if there are any differences in how you are relating to these different groups; Are you more effective with some cultures than others? Why? How can you leverage your successes with some cultural groups, so you can better adapt to dealing with others? Also, are you sharing your findings with other stores in your chain, other departments in your company or your business partners? After you ask each question, use the space below to list your strengths and areas for development for each cultural group. Use a separate sheet for each group of customers.

A. CUSTOMER CULTURAL GROUP: _____

Effective Areas

Behaviors: _____

_____

_____

_____

Attitudes: _____

_____

_____

_____

Product Or Service: _____

_____

_____

_____

Improvement Areas

Behaviors:
_____

_____

_____

_____

Attitudes:
_____

_____

_____

_____

Product Or Service:
_____

_____

_____

_____

B. EMPLOYEE CULTURAL GROUP: _____

Effective Areas

Behaviors:
_____

_____

_____

_____

Attitudes:
_____

_____

_____

_____

Product Or Service: _____

_____

_____

_____

Improvement Areas

Behaviors: _____

_____

_____

_____

Attitudes: _____

_____

_____

_____

Product Or Service: _____

_____

_____

_____

4) Change Management: Goal Setting With *Start, Stop, Continue*

By this point, you have had a chance to assess yourself, your team and your products or services and have undoubtedly thought of some changes to make. You've come this far; now don't let your ideas dry up and blow away. Let's take a look at a strategy that will enable you to take the learning points and theories from this book and turn them into action items and success. I have implemented this next exercise in companies around the world and am constantly amazed by the successful results. The beauty lies in its simplicity and, when done on a regular basis, will help you and your team maintain your focus on your change initiatives. As with any change, it takes time to move from deliberate, purposeful action, the "beginner stage" to the "advanced stage" where things are done automatically.

This exercise is called Start, Stop, Continue (SSC) and can be done in a variety of ways, but the end result is always the same: focusing on the goal, then holding people accountable leads to success. If you are embarking on a series of changes, it is vitally important to identify *what* needs to be changed, *how* it will be changed, *who* is responsible for the change and *when* the change will occur. The other wonderful component of this exercise is that it doesn't focus exclusively on what is wrong or what needs to be changed. In the *Continue* column, you are able to identify areas of strength, what you are doing right, so it serves as a way to balance out the approach.

SSC is simple to explain and simple to use:

Start: What do you as an individual, team or company want to *Start* doing that will be an improvement over your current approach? What can you do that is more culturally sensitive?

Stop: What have you identified as culturally unacceptable, either for your customer or employee groups, that you need to *Stop*?

Continue: What are your strengths? How can you ensure the maintenance of these strengths in light of the changes you are planning to make. It helps you avoid "throwing the baby out with the bathwater" that so often accompanies change initiatives.

Rolling out SSC can be as simple or as complicated as you want to make it. For the Start and Stop areas, after identifying *what* needs to be changed, be sure to identify the *how* it can be changed, *who* will be responsible and by *when* it will be accomplished. Then, on a regular basis, re-visit each. I've seen this done in a variety of ways, from daily one-to-one meetings, to regular staff meetings that always incorporate SSC into the agenda. It is quite amazing to see how organizations can make positive change when these simple questions are asked: "Last week in our staff meeting, we identified items one, two and three as definite 'Start' behaviors. Have we started them yet? If not, what or who is in the way?" Or, "Last week in our staff meeting, we identified items X,Y and Z as must 'Stop' attitudes. Are we seeing any progress here? If not, what or who is perpetuating them?" Once a "Start" has been accomplished, add another. Once a "Stop" has been eliminated, add another.

The key is to keep chipping away at those "Starts" and "Stops," while maintaining your strengths, your "Continues." However, in order to obtain the maximum benefits, you have to agree to the following ground rules:

- Be Creative, Let Others Be Creative
- Challenge Everything: Policies, Procedures, Products, And Corporate History
- Be Able To Defend Anything: Policies, Procedures, Products, Corporate History
- If Necessary, Break The Mold And Start Again

As you can see in the worksheet on pages 251 through 253, SSC can be divided into both short and long-term goals, and it is important to do both. Some short-term goals can be attained within hours and identifying these is a valuable exercise. Here's the catch: As a starting point, choose some short-term goals that can be attained. There should be absolutely no excuses for not accomplishing them. There can be no political barriers, there can be no resource barriers (human, monetary, facilities, equipment and so on). For example, remember the chapter on how to change your English to make it more understandable for non-native speakers? Choose one of the strategies listed as a skill recommended to become a better listener or speaker, and then practice it. If you do this, you will undoubtedly improve your ability to communicate across cultural divides. Yet, many people who have been exposed to these simple skills fail to use them and don't improve. Why? Well, there are many reasons, yet not a few are self-imposed. "Not enough time" or "I already communicate effectively." Unfortunately, one's self importance, ego, inflexibility or ignorance are the only barriers to improvement and these are not acceptable. The reality is that anyone or any department with a *desire* to change can accomplish a short-term "Start" or "Stop" goal. That is the beauty of this step. It leads to success and motivation. It prepares individuals and teams to tackle the more complicated, long-term SSC goals that, by their nature are full of obstacles and take more time to handle.

To help you get started, take a look at the topics listed on the next page. If the functions or topics listed reside in your organization, consider the following questions:

•Do these support your multicultural leadership and service efforts?

• If so, how can you ensure they are Continued?

• If not, what do you or your team need to Stop doing or Start doing to improve your approach?

A PRIMER FOR DISCUSSION: DO THESE SUPPORT YOUR MULTICULTURAL LEADERSHIP AND SERVICE EFFORTS?

• Training Programs
• Service Reliability
• Performance Reviews
• Incentive Programs
• Leadership Style
• Training Follow-Up
• Relationships between Cultural Groups
• Recruiting Strategy
• Cost of Service
• Work Environment
• Vision/Mission/Culture
• Crisis Management
• Work Schedules
• Message Consistency
• Sense of Urgency
• Office Automation
• Equipment and Supplies
• Employee/Customer Comfort, Convenience & Safety
• Customer/Employee Benefits
• Empowerment (Does staff know how to handle every conceivable situation)
• Feedback Mechanisms (Does management get "filtered" or unfiltered data from team?)
• Balance of doing "your job" and human relations
• Customer/Employee Surveys (consistently sent out, then acted upon?)

This is just a starting point. Create your own list that will generate interest and discussion. Remember to start out with some short-term, individual goals that can be easily attained. As with any approach, consistency is the key. Your next step should be to repeat this type of exercise on a regular basis, on your own as well as with your team.

Start: Stop: Continue:
Think of and list as many ways you would like to improve your ability to consistently provide exceptional service to your internal and external customers who come from diverse cultural backgrounds. What can you do that is an improvement over current practices? What should you *start, stop* or *continue*? How can you continually outperform yourself to exceed the needs of your multicultural customers and employees? Challenge *every* existing area of your approach to your job, your team or the organization as a whole.

I. Short-Term: Your Leadership Style

Start: _____

_____

_____

Stop: _____

_____

_____

Continue: _____

_____

_____

I. Long-Term: Your Leadership Style

Start: _____

_____

_____

Stop: _____

_____

_____

Continue: _____

_____

_____

II. Short-Term: Your Department

Start: _____

_____

_____

Stop: _____

_____

_____

Continue: _____

_____

_____

II. Long-Term: Your Department

Start:
_____

_____

_____

Stop:
_____

_____

_____

Continue:
_____

_____

_____

[1] Bennis, Warren and Thomas, Robert. *Geeks & Geezers: How Era, Values and Defining Moments Shape Leaders.* Harvard Business School Press, August, 2002.